THE
PATH
TO
WEALTH

MAY McCARTHY

THE
PATH
TO
WEALTH

Hier⊕phantpublishing

Cover design by Adrian Morgan
Cover art by Mopic | Shutterstock
Book design by Jane Hagaman

Hierophant Publishing
8301 Broadway, Suite 219
San Antonio, TX 78209
888-800-4240
www.hierophantpublishing.com

If you are unable to order this book from your local bookseller, you may order directly from the publisher.

Library of Congress Control Number: 2014958927

ISBN: 978-1-938289-59-0

10 9 8 7 6 5 4 3 2 1

Printed on acid-free paper in the United States of America

*To my sister, Sharon Ramey, who has been
my great teacher, dear friend, and valued mentor.
This book would not have been possible
without your loving support.*

Your time is limited, so don't waste it living someone else's life. Don't be trapped by dogma, which is living with the results of other people's thinking. Don't let the noise of others' opinions drown out your own inner voice. And most important, have the courage to follow your heart and intuition.

—Steve Jobs

The intuitive mind is a sacred gift and the rational mind is a faithful servant. We have created a society that honors the servant and has forgotten the gift.

—Albert Einstein

Contents

Preface

Business can be a game of fun and prosperity. I've proved this over the past thirty-one years as I've built six companies, many of which were successful and profitable multi-million-dollar businesses. My desire is that you learn how to do the same—how to experience more fun and success in your work and your life. In this book, you'll learn the seven-step daily practice I used to create financial abundance in my life. This is what I want for you too, and it's the reason I wrote this book.

As you practice the steps in this book, you'll have new experiences that increase your fun, ease, and success. You'll gain insight about your purpose. You'll discover how to successfully navigate ups and downs in your business and your life. Perhaps best of all, you'll eliminate old behaviors that have kept you from the experiences you really want.

This book describes universal principles you can use to create a true partnership with the all-knowing power that is prepared to guide you. This power is within you and knows what is necessary for you to receive what you want.

You'll learn the job descriptions for both yourself and your new partner, freeing you to do your part while trusting that your partner is handling the real heavy lifting. You'll no longer have to carry the burden of doing everything yourself. You have a partner that can help you.

Different backgrounds and traditions use different names to describe the all-knowing power of the universe—Infinite Intelligence, the Universe, Spirit, God, Truth, etc. Whatever you call this power, I believe it is the same universal energy that flows through us all. Because I believe there is an intelligent and divine source that created the one and only you, you must by your very nature have something to offer the world that is unique and remarkable. I believe this higher power wants to support your efforts and enable you to receive all that you want easily and joyfully. You deserve to have these good things. This book teaches you the simple steps to receive the good that you desire.

For the purpose of this book, I will call this power the Chief Spiritual Officer, or the "CSO," but remember that you may refer to it in whatever language is comfortable for you. No matter what you call this power, I can assure you that partnering with it in a daily practice will help you gain a higher level of success and greater enjoyment in all areas of your life.

Let me tell you why I chose the name Chief Spiritual Officer for the all-knowing, universal power that wants to help me succeed. In my position as a CEO, I surround myself with other "c-suite" executives whose advice I value. This includes my chief financial officer, who advises me about the financial position and directions for our company; my chief information officer, who advises me about the technical tools our company should use and the software and products we should create and sell; and my chief operating officer, who advises me about the operations of our company, including our organizational relations, implementations, and customer service. I decided my Chief Spiritual Officer would have the most valuable advice for me for all areas of my business, and I placed it on the top of my organizational chart and meet with it every day.

As you move through the book, you'll be exposed to a number of universal principles and tools involving your words, thoughts, and emotions. You'll read the experiences and outcomes of myself and others as we've partnered with the CSO using these tools. You'll discover that the CSO as your partner provides wisdom, guidance, and direction to enable you to achieve your goals. If you commit to partnering with the CSO and following the direction it provides, you will receive what you want.

There is good in store for you. You can have it all while experiencing fun, ease, success, and financial freedom. I'm delighted to join you on your journey.

Introduction

Meet the CSO
(Chief Spiritual Officer)

I have been blessed to experience wonderful business opportunities and successes, but I didn't do all the work and planning alone. Others helped me—and, more importantly, the all-knowing power of the universe that I call the CSO helped me. This power guided me to do what I needed to do to receive what I wanted. All I had to do was trust the direction I received and work with the CSO as my partner.

I have been a founding member of many successful businesses since 1982 in a wide range of industries, including fashion retail, telecommunications, health care, IT software, and inventory management systems. The largest company was staffed by over 250 employees with revenues that exceeded $100 million.

As my trust in the universal power matured and I grew in my partnership with the CSO, my success and prosperity increased immensely. The work also became easier. Because I felt increased peace and happiness, the work didn't seem as burdensome, and at times it even felt like I was actually doing less.

Within a year of selling my last company, I felt guided to speak publically and teach workshops about the universal principles. I designed a curriculum that shared how to partner with the CSO. Students completing the workshops tell of realizing the same wonderful benefits that I do when I'm in partnership with the CSO.

What I have learned, and what you'll soon discover as you take on and practice the steps in this book, is that the CSO is completely trustworthy. The CSO and I each have a job description and responsibility in the partnership and are competent to do what is ours to do. How does the process work? Put simply, you decide what you want and thank the CSO for it in advance. The CSO's job is to create the path to get to the good you've defined and provide you with direction to get there, one step at a time. Your job is to follow each step and sometimes ask for further direction if you need it along the way. As this process unfolds, you receive the good that you desire—and celebrate!

When you do your job and the CSO does its job, you will receive what you want. I've proven repeatedly that all things are possible if I just do my job and allow the CSO to do its job. You can experience this, too!

My desire is to introduce you to the daily practice techniques that I've developed and ask that you practice them for a minimum of thirty days. I believe that thirty days allows the new student to feel fully committed to the daily routine. Consistent application in regular doses is also a necessary piece of forming any new habit. At the end of the thirty days, you can continue the practice, modifying steps as necessary to make your relationship with the CSO more personal.

Every successful business leader knows that a daily planning session and goal review with top management is vital to a vibrant and profitable company. Spiritual leaders agree. A daily spiritual practice is recommended in ancient and modern religious writings alike, as well as in houses of worship worldwide. Successful people (in all areas of life) set specific goals, review them in a consistent manner, focus on their skills, and act on opportunities to achieve their goals. Countless examples tell us how daily practice methods can bring the blessings we seek, and now this daily CSO practice will help you remain consistent and focused on your financial goals.

As a successful businesswoman, I understand that consistent planning is vital. I plan my day, week, month, and year, and I am committed to arriving at every appointment on time. In order to be consistent with my daily practice of goal setting and partnering with the CSO, I scheduled a daily meeting for us on my calendar at the same time every morning. I informed all coworkers, friends, and family members that I would be unavailable during that time. I recommend that you do the same.

The daily practice I'll be introducing you to has a very specific method I've adapted from business experience and religious tradition. I've also added other steps that I developed myself as I matured in my trust of the universal principles. Since every one of us is unique, any relationship with the power of the universe within us will be unique as well. As you practice the steps and meet with the CSO daily, you will begin to figure out what techniques for connection work best for you.

In the following chapters, we will discuss each of the seven daily steps that will bring you increased success and financial freedom. As you discover how the seven steps work, you'll have new experiences that may appear to be too good to be true or that can't easily be explained. You may feel an urge to drive across town to a location that makes no sense or to call someone you haven't thought of in years. Thoughts, hunches, urges, and other impulses that aren't easily explained are going to surface while using this practice. This is normal and all part of the journey. Don't spend too much time trying to figure out why this is happening. The book will teach you how to pay attention to these messages, interpret them correctly, and act on the direction to achieve your goals.

You will experience seeming miracles on your path that you never thought possible, all with less effort and more fun, satisfaction, and success, with the CSO as your partner.

It wasn't an accident that you picked up this book. This is part of the universal power's plan to guide you toward the good that you desire and deserve. Now is the time for you to receive your good. Let the CSO take part in your life and direct you each and every step of the way to receive all that you desire.

Part One

Commit to a Daily Practice of These Seven Steps

For the things we have to learn before we can do them, we learn by doing them; e.g., men become builders by building and lyre players by playing the lyre.
—Aristotle, *Nicomachean Ethics*

Human nature loves variety. Often, therefore, we look negatively at any kind of repetition or routine. In the film *The Karate Kid*, a master of the martial arts has his young student wax cars or sand floors each day, performing the same circular hand movements all day long. The boy doesn't like it and complains, "This isn't karate." But this discipline prepares the boy to handle the more challenging lessons taught later. He learns to remain calm in the face of adversity and focus on the goals that he wants to achieve.

Just like the scenes from *The Karate Kid*, daily practice is a discipline that lays the foundation for you to work through any future challenges with a sense of calm and peace and prepares you to receive the good you want. After the first few days of the practice, you may receive signs that point you in the direction of your good. Eventually, you'll look forward to using the practice each day. By day thirty, you will be well on your way to mastering and trusting the universal power of the CSO as your partner.

The first four steps in your daily practice take place in a meeting with your CSO each morning. I suggest allowing about thirty minutes for this meeting, depending on your goals and what you put on the meeting agenda. Each meeting should take place in a comfortable and quiet space that you've created in your home, with meeting tools such as journals, pens, and books that put you in a receptive mood. It would be beneficial to tell your coworkers, friends, and family that you will be unavailable during this time (the same way you would if you had a meeting with another person) so that you will not be interrupted.

I have been successfully using all the elements of this meeting process for over three decades and have formulated them into the specific format presented here over the last ten years. This process has produced even greater success than I imagined. I will provide more detail about each step in later chapters, so if questions come up while you're reading the meeting format that follows, write them down and set them aside. They will most likely be answered as you continue reading the book. And remember, this format is a guide—you may feel moved to alter this agenda slightly to suit your individual needs.

The following example meeting begins at 6:00 A.M.:

The CSO Meeting

Date: _____. The CSO and I attended the meeting.

6:00 A.M.: **Step 1**: Read something spiritual and uplifting to get in a receptive mood.

I read: _____

6:10 A.M.: **Step 2**: Write out gratitude statements in a letter to the CSO. Include those things that I am grateful for and those that I want as though they are already manifest in my life. (Use a notebook for your daily CSO letter.)

6:20 A.M.: **Step 3**: Speak as I read my letter out loud with emotion.

6:25 A.M.: **Step 4**: Imagine, think about, and feel grateful for all that I've listed as my desires as though I already have them. What does it feel like to have them now? How do I look having those things or experiences?

I may hear or feel some guidance from the CSO as a direction to do something. If I do, I'll write it below:

_____

_____

I may or may not hear or feel any guidance about what steps I should take next while I am in the meeting. That's okay. If I do, I'll follow directions or ask for another lead.

6:30 A.M.: Meeting adjourned.

The next two steps take place throughout the day.

Step 5: Watch every moment of the day for a sign or some intuitive direction to take the next step toward my desired good. Instead of simply hoping, expect that these signs will show up; and when they do, don't overanalyze the instructions.

Today I will follow the intuitive leads, flashes, and hunches that I received and will list them below:

_____

_____

Step 6: Celebrate and express gratitude in a joyful way when something good happens that is related to what I want by calling a friend or texting a relative to celebrate.

Today I celebrated the good of

_____

with

_____ .

Note any demonstrations as signs that my good is showing up. Nothing is too small.

I received the following demonstration today:

_____ .

The final step happens at night, just before you go to sleep.

Step 7: As I prepare to settle into bed at night, I say out loud gratitude statements for anything that I can remember off the top of my head that happened that day. (Use your notes if you'd like to be more specific when you do this.)

After thanking the CSO for these things, I commit to forgiving anyone, including myself, for anything that's been done in the past or present that needs to be cleared out of my life. (pages 79–80 for a sample forgiveness mantra.)

If you're not able to do this final step of the practice in bed, do it somewhere else in your home before going to bed. This step is important and sets your mind on having more freedom in your life and makes room for the good that you desire to be received.

There's no predetermined amount of time for each step on the meeting agenda—this schedule is meant to be suggestive only. Each step will take as long as you and the CSO decide to take with them. As you practice the steps consistently, the process will become easier for you. Until then, keep the outline of the practice with your meeting tools for reference. Don't rush through your meeting. Appreciate and maximize the time that you're spending with the CSO.

Being Consistent

If you want consistent results, you have to be consistent with your practice. When I practice consistently, I experience my good more steadily, without emotional and financial highs and lows. I feel more peace, fulfillment, and joy, along with freedom, success, and prosperity. You can achieve anything that you want simply by having a consistent practice that will support you in that goal.

Prior to learning how important consistency was, I would practice these techniques only during a crisis. When my life was going well—good health, calm relationships, increasing finances, goal achievement—I would get lazy and inconsistent with my practice. I'd miss a day or two here and there and not rely as much on the all-knowing universal power for help. Then, a curveball (loss of customers, reduced income, relationship problems, illness) would cross my plate—and I would jump back into a daily practice with a sense of urgency to regain peace and stability. This was stressful—and unnecessary.

When I've asked students, friends, and colleagues if this has happened to them, the answer across the board has been a resounding "yes." The importance of being consistent is something everyone starts out having to learn by doing. My swings through crisis and drama were emotional roller-coaster rides that I had unconsciously chosen to stay on for several years.

For example, when I was in my late twenties and before I had a consistent daily practice, I helped start a business. Everything was going great. Up until that time, I had practiced goal setting and affirmative prayer techniques only when I felt I needed to. This usually happened with fervor after some crisis or challenge had presented itself or when I had a specific performance goal that I wanted to reach.

Since all was going well in my business and I was very busy with clients, I became less consistent in my affirmative prayer practice for myself, our business, and the employees. Instead, I used the time to manage our overseas clients. Within a couple months, a huge challenge appeared. Our key technical employee got into some serious legal trouble, which could have resulted in jail time for him. Our business might experience a giant setback without this employee. I immediately felt scared and imagined all sorts of worst-case-scenario outcomes. We'd lose our business, he'd be in jail—or worse.

I also knew that an adverse effect of being panicked and filled with fear was that it prevented me from getting the help I needed from the power of the universe. A fearful mind-set does not allow any room for the CSO to work. Fear and doubt created a block in the channel of communication, and I wasn't able to hear any directions to guide me. As part of my fear, I thought a lot about worst-case scenarios.

I couldn't get these images out of my mind. I lost a lot of sleep over the next two weeks. I was a wreck. At the point of physical exhaustion, I finally allowed myself to surrender, be still, and start using affirmative prayer techniques that relied on universal truths. I focused my words, thoughts, and emotions deliberately on what I wanted and stopped giving so much attention to the problem and outcomes that I didn't want.

This proved to be more difficult than I expected. My mind kept wandering to the worst possible outcomes. I wrote out on paper and recited out loud affirmative statements that I could use when troubling thoughts entered my mind:

"All adverse appearances dissipate, and a good outcome for all is revealed now."

"I give thanks that this legal matter is now dissolved for the benefit of all."

"I cast all burdens of fear on the spirit within and I go free to see good results appear in this situation."

"Everything is possible in divine mind, and this legal situation disintegrates before my eyes; all are free."

I pasted notes around me with reminders about how the universal truths worked and reassurance that nothing was impossible. I kept reciting affirmative statements even though I was still scared and filled with doubt. Writing and speaking were the only way out.

In James Allen's book *As a Man Thinketh*, we learn how our thoughts determine reality whether or not we are conscious of it. He explains that our underlying beliefs shape our circumstances, our self-definitions, and our destinies. I believe that thoughts are as powerful as the use of words. When we add emotions to words and thoughts, we create a powerful force that makes us magnetic to that about which we are speaking, thinking, and feeling. You get to choose where to put your focus. You get to choose what you will receive. Choose to focus on what you want and you will get it.

I knew intellectually that whatever I decided to focus my attention on would surely manifest, but while I was gripped with fear I had trouble feeling the truth of what I was saying.

In spite of this, I continued to repeat the affirmative words out loud hundreds of times per day. I needed to drown out the negative thoughts that would attack my mind.

I claimed that this situation was not too big for the power of the universe to handle and that there could be an outcome that was good for everyone. I spoke my words for "right action" and knew that the attorney we had hired to help our employee was equipped to do the very best job. After six weeks of this daily practice, I started to feel a glimmer of peace. I knew that it truly was possible for the situation to turn out well for everyone involved. As you can imagine, our employee was very scared during this time. I asked him to state affirmative prayers for a good verdict as well.

And yes, it all did turn out well. Our employee was sentenced to a work release program, which allowed him to go to and from work and home. He was immensely grateful that he wasn't in jail and for the legal help we had provided. As a result, he worked long hours for us to channel his creativity into designing even better products than he had previously. Our company and customers received terrific new products from him, and the courts and prison system didn't have to incur additional expense to care for another inmate. I believe that the universal power was activated by our collective statements to orchestrate the best solution possible.

There will always be distressing situations in life that we can't control. But if we're prepared, we don't have to experience debilitating distress. I didn't have any control over how our employee had ended up in trouble with the law. What I could control were my own words and thoughts. I could focus on a positive outcome in order to maintain my own peace. The use of affirmative statements got me to a place of peace where I could see the possibility of good outcomes, but if I had remembered to keep up with my daily practices and been consistent, I might have gotten to a place of peace sooner, rather than waiting until I was exhausted from fear.

Please understand this critical piece of the story: *I didn't specifically state the exact outcome that I wanted; rather, I affirmed with gratitude that there could be an outcome that was good for all involved.* Each time a negative thought popped up, I obliterated it with an affirmation of gratitude. I armed myself with these statements by writing them down and placing them in easy-to-access locations. After several weeks of reciting them, the feelings followed. I started to believe that a good outcome could be everyone's experience. I recognized a wonderful lesson here. The power of the universe is always available, but it works best for me when I'm at peace and untroubled. To maintain a level of peace and strength, a consistent practice is required.

In hindsight, I see that I was repeating a pattern I had experienced many times before: an emotional roller-coaster ride filled with crisis and drama. Now let's look back at your life for a moment. Have you experienced the same difficult situation repeatedly? What has shown up more than once that you'd like to change? For example, have you had several jobs where someone else was promoted over you? Have you had relationships with superiors, coworkers, or clients that started out great and then turned into something that was filled with tension? Have you worried about your income and had to go into debt just to make ends meet more often than you'd like? Have you felt overwhelmed at work and busy all the time, leaving no free time for you to have fun?

In all these examples, the problems have become the focus of your attention. Very little time has been left to allow for the good outcomes that you desire. With this shift in perspective, you can choose to make a change and use gratitude and affirmative statements along with the CSO practice to develop a lasting peace and attract the good outcomes that you want.

This peace I have found is available to you, and a daily meeting with the CSO can help get you there. With practice, you'll learn to focus on what you want and be grateful for receiving it. Even if you don't have these things yet, be grateful for perfect, fulfilling, satisfying work that rewards you financially and recognizes your great contributions. Be grateful for the harmonious work environment with all your superiors, coworkers, and clients. Be grateful for the abundance and prosperity that are yours now, which are more than enough to allow you to easily pay all your bills and expenses each month. Be grateful that you have a balanced, happy life with enough time for you to do the things that bring you great joy. The more gratitude you place in your goals, the more quickly you will see them come to fruition.

Since using this daily CSO practice, I don't have the severe emotional, physical, and financial ups and downs that I used to. I work with the CSO daily and experience more of what I want instead of pleading with the power of the universe to help me when something goes wrong. I am now happier and more financially free. You can be too.

In the following pages, we'll go over each of the agenda items in the daily CSO meeting in greater detail so that you can gain a better understanding of each one's importance to the process. Remember that although this is a journey of understanding, we learn things best by doing them. Your understanding will grow as you practice these seven steps. Don't worry if you don't fully grasp everything right away. Keep up the daily practice and the understanding will follow.

Exercise

Think of a challenging situation in your past when you've asked (or begged) the spirit of the universe, God, divine intelligence, an all-knowing power, or whatever you might call this presence, to help you. Write a description of the help you wanted and how you asked for it. Did you receive the help you wanted? Did it arrive easily? If you could have avoided the problem by dedicating thirty minutes a day for thirty days prior to the problem occurring, would you have taken the time to do the prevention work? Do you want to make a change in your life that reduces problems and increases the amount of good you want to receive in your life?

Write your statement of commitment to have the CSO as your partner. Add a statement of agreement to attend the daily meeting and to welcome and receive more of the good that you want to experience into your life.

Step 1

Read Something Inspirational

We read to know that we are not alone.
—C. S. Lewis, *Shadowlands*

Now that you've made the commitment to enter into a daily practice with the CSO, you will create and follow the meeting agenda each day. The first agenda item is to read something that inspires you. Ideally, this material will strengthen your conviction that the all-knowing universal power is active and available for your benefit. During this part of the meeting, you'll begin to change your mind-set to one of infinite possibilities with the CSO as your partner.

If you were convinced that the all-knowing power of the universe were truly your partner and could guide you to receive anything that you wanted without limitation, would you agree to partner with it? To help convince you that the CSO wants to partner with you for your benefit, it's helpful to read stories about others using this power to achieve all that they want.

One of my favorite books to demonstrate how the all-knowing universal power operates is *The Game of Life and How to Play It* by Florence Scovel Shinn (1925). This small book had a transformative effect on me when my mother gave it to me for my high school graduation. I read it over many times, becoming convinced that the good results others had experienced could be mine as well. I repeated the affirmations in the book to proclaim what I wanted. As a result of following the book's lessons, I graduated from college with honors in three years, cofounded and grew a business to 250 employees while going to school full-time, and had a stable and loving relationship. I practiced the principles while participating in organized religion with family and loved ones without any conflict.

The stories I read in Shinn's book, along with other books based on universal power principles, helped convince me that I could use this power for my benefit and receive all the good that I desired. Put simply, I learned I have to proclaim what I want, believe that I can have it, and welcome and receive the good into my life. This will work for you as well.

Many great authors describe how people from all walks of life are affected by the power of the universe. As people intentionally practice the universal power principles, they experience improved health, finances, and relationships. These stories will inspire you to believe that any good is available for you to receive. With the CSO as your partner, you're sure to bring it into your experience. Reading something inspiring will put your mind into a receptive state, which makes it an ideal first step for your daily CSO meeting. A list of books for you to consider is provided in the appendix.

Often in the reading step of the meeting, there will be a quality or situation in the stories that strikes an emotional chord in you. This emotional connection becomes a catalyst for you to recognize this truth: What the CSO has done for others the CSO now does for me and more. Say that out loud and see how it feels. This is a great affirmative statement to keep in your wallet and desk drawer. Recite it any time another's good comes to your attention. *It will help you remember that good is as available to you as it is to others.*

There is no limit to the all-knowing power of the universe. We live in an abundant and prosperous world. As such, this abundance is available for all, and it does not diminish when someone else receives the good they desire. The idea that there is only so much good to go around is false. We should celebrate the good fortune of others. As we do so, we are activating a spiritual law of giving and receiving that allows us to become magnetic to the same or better happening for us. Others receiving their good is a sign that we can also receive our good. Bless them with positive thoughts for their good fortune, and you will also be blessed with yours.

You may not know this, but most of the successful people you read about in magazines and newspapers practice inspirational daily reading. When they read inspirational material and believe the underlying truths through their words, thoughts, and emotions, they achieve their goals. If you find out about the reading habits of some of the most successful people on the planet, you will find out that this is so. And the great news is, this universal power operates the same way for everyone. Let's look at Oprah Winfrey, who is worth over $3 billion and has been called the most influential celebrity on the planet by *Forbes* magazine. When asked about her ten favorite books, she listed *Discover the Power Within You* by Eric Butterworth and *A New Earth* by Eckhart Tolle as two of her top picks. These books helped to inspire her to become the best that she could be. Steve Jobs, one of the greatest innovators of our century, said that *Be Here Now* by Ram Dass and *Zen Mind, Beginner's Mind* by Shunryu Suzuki were two of his favorites that had transformative effects in his life.

For the reading step, one option is to choose books with short stories about real people and how the universal power has shown up to work with them for their good. It's important that you spend only five to ten minutes on the reading portion. The only purpose of this part of the practice is to set your mind on the CSO operating in and through people in successful and wonderful ways. It's ideal to add extra reading at other times of the day that supports universal truth principles, and I encourage you to do so. It will help you discard beliefs you may have that aren't serving you.

The reading part of the agenda helps you to replace any old "recordings" from your past. Perhaps others have told you that "You need a college degree to be successful." Or, "You're lazy and will never have the drive to make it big in life." Or, "You'll never be as accomplished as your cousin since he was raised in a wealthy family." Or, "As a woman, you'll never be as successful or get paid as much as a man." All those old recordings and ones like them need to be demolished!

The reading practice supports the promise that anything is possible, for anyone, at any time. All you need to do is partner with the universal power and believe that you will receive what you want. You can receive all that you require, desire, and more. Attending the CSO meeting and following the agenda are the means to move you in the direction of the good you want.

Exercise

Read the following two stories. Do you identify with either situation? Answer the questions at the end of the stories.

A woman I knew asked me why she was poor when she used to be wealthy. She used to have a large, beautiful home and gorgeous things. She always had money to do whatever she wanted and appeared carefree. While living an affluent lifestyle, she began to complain about managing her 10,000-square-foot home on the lake. She'd say, "I'm sick and tired of having to care for everything and do so much for people. I wish I lived in a room like I had in college, where there was nothing to worry about." Within a few years her life had changed dramatically, and she was living in a small apartment that she said was the size of her college room. She had talked herself into that small room with her words and beliefs.

Unfortunately, for this woman the words that she intended as jokes delivered to her an unfortunate experience. The subconscious mind has no sense of humor. We have to be very careful of the words we use. The good news is that the subconscious and universal power work both ways; we can use our words, thoughts, and emotions to attract what we want.

One of my students told me the following story about his daily practice:

The first couple days of attending the CSO meeting felt a bit like a chore. I had to wake up earlier than normal to fit the morning meeting into my schedule, and that made me tired by the end of the day. But I did it, and . . . on the fourth day I woke up before the alarm and looked forward to the meeting with my CSO. I felt more energized than I had the previous mornings even though I'd gotten the same amount of sleep. I began to notice that I already had so much to be grateful for. Little demonstrations showed up, such as great parking spaces, new inquiries for our business, a coworker who appreciated some assistance, and a mention of our products in a trade magazine. I celebrated each one of these with my friends and employees. On the fifth day, I received a $10,000 new order from a company we hadn't included on our prospect list. They said another customer had told them they could buy the products they needed from us. This increase was just what I wanted!"

Consider a time when you've thought about and spoken words describing what you didn't want and had it happen anyway. What kinds of thoughts and words did you repeat leading up to that event? What words might you have used instead to support what you really wanted? When looking at the people in each story, what qualities did you recognize in yourself? Which qualities would you like to banish? Which would you like to cultivate and grow?

Step 2

Write a Gratitude Letter

What I've learned is there's a scientifically proven phenomenon that's attached to gratitude, and that if you consciously take note of what is good in your life, quantifiable benefits happen.

—Deborah Norville,
television anchor and journalist

Now that you've started your meeting and set the tone by reading inspirational literature, it's time for the second agenda item, the heart of the meeting. This is the creative part of the practice, when you widen your thoughts to all the possibilities that exist for your good.

The second step in the CSO meeting is to write out gratitude statements in a daily letter to the CSO. In this section, you'll express gratitude for what you already have and for all that you'd like to receive as though you have already received it. This is a form of goal setting with gratitude.

Gratitude improves emotional and physical health and can strengthen relationships and communities, according to author and researcher Dr. Robert Emmons. In his best-selling book *Thanks!*, Dr. Emmons backs up his claim with eight years of intensive research. He found that people who view life as a gift and consciously acquire an "attitude of gratitude" will experience multiple advantages. "Gratitude enriches human life," he writes. "It elevates, energizes, inspires and transforms. People are moved, opened and humbled through expressions of gratitude." Some strategies Dr. Emmons recommends for expressing gratitude include keeping a gratitude journal, learning prayers of gratitude, and using visual reminders.

In the CSO gratitude letter process, you'll benefit from the same results described by Dr. Emmons. You'll proclaim your gratitude in words that evoke strong uplifting emotions. This is a place to list goals and intentions that you haven't achieved yet, showing gratitude for them as if they have already manifested in your life.

As you're writing, you may also feel inspired to list goals that you hadn't thought of prior to attending the CSO meeting that day. That's perfectly fine. Consider these possibilities divinely inspired.

For example, in one of my CSO meetings I brought the concern that our company needed to reach a sales goal of $400,000 by the end of the month. My gratitude letter stated, "Thank you for the harmonious relationship that our company has with all current and future customers. I am so grateful that the right customers are being drawn to us and that we can help them in superior ways. I appreciate the $400,000 in new business that we receive by the end of the month as a fair exchange of value." This is an example of giving gratitude both for what I already had and also what I wanted to have happen.

What the CSO does with this is create the best path to the good that I desire. The CSO creates the path and orchestrates situations that allow me to make my gratitude statements true. When I practice this form of gratitude, I receive definite direction or leads from the CSO about where to be or what actions to take. Perhaps I run into a customer at a trade show and share the benefits of our products. Perhaps a prospect talks to one of my current customers and finds out that she needs what we have to offer. Perhaps the lead is to call someone the CSO brings to mind or to go somewhere at a certain time only to find a new customer there, waiting for me.

I know that the CSO will somehow create a path for my gratitude statements to become true. All you need to focus on in this step is expressing gratitude both for what you have and what you'd like as though you already have it. Then, wait for the CSO to guide you to the next step.

In the example above, I thanked the CSO for $400,000 in sales resulting from a fair exchange of value with our customers. I thanked the CSO for the $400,000 as though my company had already received it. I described with gratitude what I'd like, and in doing so I set my mind and energy vibration on that good.

Within the first week of thanking the CSO for the $400,000, a customer came to mind. I felt an impulse to call her, which I obeyed. I called her office and learned that she had left her position three months prior for a new job at a larger health system. I called her cell phone and congratulated her on her new position. She thanked me and said that she had planned to call me later that week. She wanted to implement our software and equipment technology across all her hospitals in the new health system. She had already received budget approval of the overall plan, and the hospital's first order would be over $400,000. She was ready to get started with a contract right away.

It's my belief that the CSO gave me the thought of my customer and the intuitive lead or direction to call her. The CSO created an opportunity by showing me a path to get to the good that I wanted. Perhaps my customer would have gotten sidetracked with other duties that would have prevented her from calling me that week. Or, maybe a competitor would have had a chance to call her first to suggest using their products. Since I called her, I was able to secure a contract in the time frame that I desired.

The biggest problem to receiving all that we desire is our limited belief system and our fears and doubts. "As I ask and believe, I will receive." This foundational belief has proven to be true time and time again throughout my life. It took some proof to develop this belief, and the CSO practice will provide you with the proof you need to create the same belief.

If we believe that we will receive the good we want, we will. If we have doubts and fears, which translate into a belief that we can't have something we want, we'll get that experience instead. This principle works the same way for us all. One of the most successful people I've read about is Oprah Winfrey. What's her advice? "Be thankful for what you have; you'll end up having more. If you concentrate on what you don't have, you will never, ever have enough." I agree.

In Psalm 37:4, we're told, "Take delight in the Lord, and he will give you the desires of your heart." If we make a slight change to "take delight in and be grateful to the universal power, the CSO, it will give you the desires of your heart," we can see how important a role delight and gratitude play in our receiving all that we want.

Developing the discipline of using the right words and believing that good will manifest is easier said than done. Your commitment to the daily practice will ensure that you become more aware of the power of your words. Daily

itment to using the right words and writing out grat-
le statements supports change in your belief system and
eliminates fear and doubt. It helps to keep your attention
focused on the good that you want.

In your gratitude letter, you'll pour out your foundational beliefs. As you grow in this practice and your relationship with the CSO becomes stronger, you'll build trust
in the process. Your letters will change to reflect the new
confidence that you develop. Don't measure yourself falsely
or be critical of your past at any time. Enjoy the practice
each and every new day.

Use the following framework to write your CSO gratitude
letter:

Dear CSO, I am so grateful that you're my partner in business and in life and that you guide me every step of the way
toward the good that I want.

Thank you for my . . .

List what you have and are grateful for as it relates to
work, wealth, financial freedom, health, countenance or
peace, joy, ease, love, ideas, opportunities, relationships,
and whatever else is important to you. I often also list
the qualities of the CSO that I am grateful for, and I con-

sciously affirm that I have those same qualities since the CSO created me. I believe that the CSO as universal power is responsible for all creation in the universe.

Thank you for my . . .

Write gratitude statements for what you want as though you already have it. As above, list all your desires as they relate to work, wealth, financial freedom, health, countenance or peace, joy, ease, love, ideas, opportunities, relationships, and whatever else is important to you.

In this section, I also list qualities that I want to remind myself to express toward others. I state that I love, bless, and forgive everyone and that everyone loves, blesses, and forgives me. These statements are a reminder for me that we're all created by the same universal power and there are no enemies on my pathway. I can then go deeper in my desire to appreciate everyone as a wonderful link in the chain of my good, and I can see more of the CSO in others.

I don't always feel the meaning of the words within these statements when I write them, but if I continue to write them down and proclaim them out loud with gratitude (we'll do this in the next chapter), the feelings that I want will eventually follow. This is a powerful way to set and support intentions.

k you, CSO, for your universal power operating in my life.

I note, in writing, my appreciation of the CSO working in partnership with me. I do my part to describe what I want and am grateful for. I trust the CSO to do its part in our partnership to guide and direct me toward manifesting the good that I want.

 For all this good and more, I give great thanks.

Toward the end of the letter, include a blanket statement giving thanks for everything that you've written about and more. You're deliberately including a statement of openness to allow the CSO to produce situations for more good than you've described. Often, the CSO will enable you to receive more than you want, if you let it.

 I now release these words to the law, truth, and power of the universe and know that it is done.

Just as there are laws of science such as gravity and electricity, there are universal laws like the laws of intention that we are invoking when we write a gratitude letter. When you release the words that you've written and trust that the power and laws of the universe will work, you're turning it all over to the CSO to handle its part of the partnership.

You should do nothing more to make anything happen. Wait and trust that you will be guided to take the next step toward the good that you want.

Remember, the key points are:

1. Write out gratitude statements for what you appreciate now.

2. Write out gratitude statements for what you want, as though you have already received them.

3. Recognize with gratitude that the universal power can be used to receive all that you want.

4. The CSO is your partner in life and business and enables the universal power to work on your behalf.

Here's an example of one of my letters:

Good morning, CSO. Thank you for a great sleep and for all your marvelous blessings of good. Thank you for working in me, through me, as me, and by me, showing me what to do, when to do it, and how to do it in order to experience my highest and best good in all my affairs. I am so grateful that you are Love, Peace, Health, Joy, Ease, Wisdom, and Huge, Abundant Prosperity. And, as you are these qualities and so much more, so am I. Your power created me to be the perfect expression of your creation as myself here on earth. I accept that role and am delighted that my talents are being used in meaningful, satisfying, fulfilling, fun, easy, successful, and hugely prosperous ways.

Thank you, CSO, for my business. Everyone related to my business is blessed at all times and receives our good. We work toward the success of our coworkers, customers, suppliers, vendors, and our world, and accept and receive our good. We easily and joyfully create, provide, install, implement, and support our flawless, superior, easy-to-use, and maintenance-free products and services. Our customers are happy with our products and services and tell all their peers how wonderful we are. And as a result, they buy from us, too! We are a market share leader in our industry and have a wonderful reputation. Thank you that my business easily and joyfully receives a minimum of $15 million in sales this year and that we are debt-free, cash flow positive, and profitable at all times in all ways. Thank you, CSO, that our business attracts and employs the very best team members who are for our highest and best good and who enjoy their work. We bless all others related to our business and experience success.

I love everyone and everyone loves me. I love myself and am loved. I bless everyone and everyone blesses me. I bless myself and am blessed. I forgive everyone and everyone forgives me. I forgive myself and am forgiven. I am peace with poise and confidence. I am grateful for my physically fit, trim, toned, energetic, healthy body that is eternally youthful and increasingly more beautiful, whole, and complete. Joy radiates in and through me to all in our world. I am ease and live a charmed life. All that is mine to do is done easily and joyfully, and I experience my highest and best good at all times. I am wisdom and make right decisions quickly as guided and directed by the CSO. I am huge, abundant prosperity with overflowing resources. I am rich beyond my wildest dreams, with a minimum of _____ (after taxes, please) to use and enjoy, bless others with as the CSO directs, and invest and increase. I am debt-free, cash flow positive, and profitable at all times.

Thank you, CSO, for my husband, who is my perfect loving partner. We are so blessed and happy with you at the center of our relationship. Thank you, CSO, for my family, my friends, and my wonderful kitty. They are all such treasures to me. I live my purpose—I bless others and am blessed.

For all this good and so much more, I give great thanks. I now release these words to the law and it is done. And so it is!

Love you, May

In the CSO gratitude letter, I've included what I have now as well as what I want as though I already have it. As you read my letter, you may not have been able to tell which things I had already received and which ones were to manifest in the future. At the time that I wrote this letter, our business had sold $8 million of products the previous year. I thanked the CSO in advance for the increase to $15 million in sales for the current year and followed all the CSO's directions to achieve this good. By the end of the year, we had exceeded this goal. When my company was acquired by a larger company, my personal income exceeded the goal that I'd listed as my good as well.

The process of thanking the CSO for everything as though you have already received it supports that achievement of your goals and intentions. In this step, you're required to identify what you want and put a name to it. Successful people will tell you that you can't have what you haven't named. It's like steering a boat without a desired destination. You won't get anywhere if you don't set yourself on the right course— you'll just be turning in circles.

To make sure that I stay on course, I often repeat gratitude for the good that I want in several daily letters until I achieve the goal or decide that I want something different. As part of your CSO meeting, you are to write a new letter every day. It's perfectly fine to repeat gratitude statements for things that are really important to you until they manifest, but each daily meeting should launch fresh inspiration and gratitude.

Even when things are going great and you don't have any specific thing to write about or overcome, a shorter CSO letter filled with simple gratitude is appropriate to keep you focused on your overall good. Use this time to remember that the CSO is responsible for directing you step-by-step to all the good that you desire. When everything is perfectly wonderful, write out the following at a minimum in your daily CSO meeting: "Thank you, CSO, for all my good, including perfect health, wealth, happiness, and the fulfilling use of my talents. Thank you for your love and wisdom guiding and directing me to do that which is mine to do to receive the good that I desire. All related to me and my endeavors is affected positively by it."

This occasional simple gratitude prayer supports the other steps of the daily practice. You're expecting the CSO to tell you what to do so that you can do it and receive higher and greater good in wonderful and remarkable ways. It's time for you to go from good to greater good with the CSO as your partner.

Exercise

Write out a CSO letter using the following guide:

Dear CSO,

Thank you for my . . .

(List what you have and are grateful for.)

1. _____

2. _____

3. _____

4. _____

Thank you for my . . .

(List what you want as gratitude statements, as though you already have them.)

1. _____

2. _____

3. _____

4. _____

Thank you, CSO, for your universal power operating in my life.

For all this good and more, I give great thanks.

I now release these words to the law, truth, and power of the universe and know that it is done.

With gratitude and love,

(Your name)

Speak with Emotion

Be impeccable with your Word. Speak with integrity. Say only what you mean. Avoid using the Word to speak against yourself or to gossip about others. Use the power of your Word in the direction of truth and love.
—Don Miguel Angel Ruiz, *The Four Agreements*

Now that you've completed your gratitude letter to the CSO, you should be experiencing an elevated energy level and a more positive frame of mind. By having gratitude for receiving what you want, you've created greater happiness within yourself. You can now move to the next step in the meeting and read your CSO gratitude letter out loud.

Hearing yourself speak your words out loud anchors them more fully in your consciousness. Research done by Colin MacLeod and his colleagues in the May 2010 issue of the *Journal of Experimental Psychology* suggests that we remember ideas better when we speak them out loud. When you add emotional emphasis to your words, you're providing instructions to your subconscious to believe that the words are true and must be transformed into substantial form.

In Napoleon Hill's book *Think and Grow Rich*, he discusses the subconscious mind. "It receives, and files, sense impressions or thoughts, regardless of their nature. You may voluntarily plant in your subconscious mind any plan, thought, or purpose which you desire to translate into its physical or monetary equivalent. The subconscious acts first on the dominating desires which have been mixed with emotional feeling, such as faith." Hill goes on to say, "You cannot entirely control your subconscious mind, but you can voluntarily hand over to it any plan, desire, or purpose which you wish transformed into concrete form." In the CSO letter, you've taken action through writing to voluntarily hand over what you wish transformed into realized good. Now it's time to read these intentions out loud and further impress them upon the subconscious.

Speak your entire CSO letter out loud with emotion to reinforce your belief that you will receive the good that you want. Allow these statements to be "transformed into concrete form." Change your emotional energy through gratitude to become a beacon for your desires to find you. The reading out loud process starts the transformation to make you a magnet for those things that you want. Your vibration and energy elevate to equal that of the things that you desire.

More than twenty-five years ago, I made a decision to add the speaking step to my daily practice. In doing so, the intuitive leads that I got from the CSO arrived with more clarity and the good that I desired arrived much sooner. Before that time, I would read affirmative statements to myself silently when I went to the gym in the morning. As I would read on the exercise bike, I'd get distracted watching others go by, seeing the headlines on the news, and thinking about situations at work that needed my attention. I would sometimes read the same affirmative lines more than once and not retain any true meaning from them.

One morning I made a change. I decided that I wanted to more fully believe the statements of truth, so I started reading them out loud (in a soft voice that only I could hear). When I read out loud, I don't get distracted as easily, and I retain more of the information. By adding emotion to the affirmative statements, as though there was no question that they were true, I felt more energized and began to notice more opportunities that related to the truth statements.

On several mornings at the gym, I had been affirming, "Large sums of money come to me quickly, easily, and effortlessly, with grace and in perfect ways. I now have a minimum increase of $2,000 to easily pay for my vacation to Europe." One afternoon at work a few weeks later, I opened my bank statement. It turned out I had $2,000 more than I thought I had. I looked for the reason why and couldn't find a record of a deposit. I asked my sister to go over my last six months of statements with me to see if she could find a reason for the additional $2,000 in my account. She couldn't. I called the bank to confirm the balance they showed in my account. They confirmed it was there. I waited another forty-five days to see if the bank would recognize that some sort of error had been made. A notice didn't come. I figured by then that this must have been an answer to my prayer, so I used the money to pay for my trip to Europe. It was a fabulous trip filled with great fun and wonderful memories.

It's possible that I had made a mathematical error earlier in the year and the money had always been there, and that the $2,000 difference only became evident to me that month. Or, perhaps it was a gift from the bank of the universe. It made no difference to me. I wanted to go to Europe, and I was open to receiving the $2,000 that I needed in whatever way was best. I'm happy that I got it.

Here's what I believe is happening when you speak your words out loud. As you use your thoughts, words, and emotions in harmony with each other, you put yourself in a position to attract what you've focused your attention on. You become magnetic to your good and start to see opportunities and possibilities. This daily CSO practice helps you to put your thoughts, words, and emotions in alignment. Speaking "thank you" statements out loud also generates feelings of joy and happiness. Your energy level shifts to be on a similar level with what you want and where you are focusing your attention.

Barbara Fredrickson is a researcher of positive psychology at the University of North Carolina. In her 2008 paper "Open Hearts Build Lives: Positive Emotions, Induced through Loving-Kindness Meditation, Build Consequential Personal Resources," she claims, "When you are experiencing positive emotions like joy, contentment, and love, you will see more possibilities in your life . . . Positive emotions broaden your sense of possibility and open your mind up to more options." With a sense of happiness, you'll begin to see more options and be more aware of the leads from the CSO that direct you to the good you want.

We speak with emotion all the time, often without noticing how it's affecting our lives. We are either speaking for what we want or speaking for something we don't want. Either will manifest in our lives as we vibrate to it through our speech and emotions.

For example, I could say, "I wish I didn't arrive late for my appointments" or "I always arrive on time to my appointments." Say each of these statements out loud and notice how you feel when saying each of them. One is positive and higher energy, and one is negative and lower energy. We have the power to change our speech to be more positive and higher energy. In doing so, we will become more of a magnet to those things that vibrate at the higher energy level. It's a way to focus less on what you don't want and more on what you do want.

Test this yourself to see what happens. Say out loud, "I don't want to continue to feel busy, overwhelmed, and overworked in my job" (what you don't want). Now say, "I am so grateful for the ease and fun that I have with my work" (what you do want). Do you notice an energy level difference? How does your body respond to each of these statements?

As you read your gratitude letter with emotion, check in with yourself to confirm that you're using word choices that focus on what you want. When you do this, you're preparing yourself to see more opportunities to make your statements come true. As an added bonus, you can't speak out loud words for your good while thinking thoughts of doubt. It's impossible to do both at the same time. I've learned that the spoken word always wins out.

For example, in my previous business we once signed a contract with a beta customer that required us to install our newly developed software and automated shelving equipment within six months. At the beginning of month five, our equipment supplier gave us a notice of a six-week delay in delivering the equipment. I became nervous. Our customer could cancel the contract for this delay. Instead of focusing on the problem and attracting the outcome that I didn't want, I began to use my spoken words to thank my CSO for creating an even better solution for all. Every time negative thoughts came to mind, *I affirmed out loud that the all-knowing power of the universe as my CSO could turn this situation into something good.* I proved once again to myself that I couldn't think negative thoughts while saying positive statements out loud.

Within two weeks of this practice, my software design engineer suggested that we modify our software to allow our solution to work with stationary shelving instead of only with the automated shelving that was delayed by the supplier. We could also supply our customer with temporary stationary shelving so that they could operate on the date that we promised, and then replace it with the automated equipment when it arrived.

This solution not only helped our customer meet their deadline, it also allowed us to serve several more of their locations that we had previously discounted as being too small and unable to afford the automated shelving. This helped dozens of other smaller customers as well to receive the benefits of our software solution. The equipment delay enabled us to create a better solution that was of greater benefit to a larger number of customers than we thought possible. And, our company was blessed with a significant increase in revenue.

The spoken word is an incredibly powerful tool for shaping the world we live in. If your energy level has been low or you've been receiving what you don't want, examine the words that you're using. Some of the words and phrases that you use may be the result of training from a young age. I know a man who used the phrase "I'll be damned" when learning something new. He learned it from his father and didn't recognize the power in that expression. His life did reflect some "damning" and hardship. Since attending my workshop, this man has consciously worked to change that phrase to something that gives him a higher level of energy. Sometimes I'll hear him say, "I'll be blessed!" when he hears about something new. He is now living with more of the things that he wants manifesting in his life.

Listen to the words you speak and evaluate whether they are helping or hindering your progress toward the good that you want. You have the power to choose words that will empower you. You don't have to allow anything in your past or present to choose your words for you. You don't have to allow any past performance to dictate your future demonstrations. The power to choose is yours alone.

I'm delighted that you're now choosing to gain the knowledge necessary to cocreate the life that you want with your partner, the CSO.

Exercise

Speak this statement out loud while smiling: "I am a wonderful [salesperson/boss/coworker/friend] and have healthy relationships." Now, think of a business or personal relationship in your life that isn't as healthy as you'd like or where you are experiencing some strife. Repeat the statement of truth above out loud with a smile ten times and try to think of the unhealthy relationship at the same time that you're speaking. What happens? Can you do it easily? How does forcing yourself to smile while speaking affect the way your body feels? How does it affect the way you feel about this person?

Step 4

Imagine Experiencing Your Good

Visualize this thing that you want. See it, feel it, believe *in it. Make your mental blueprint, and begin to build!*
—Robert Collier, *The Secret of the Ages*

At this point in the daily meeting, you should be feeling very upbeat and positive. You've read uplifting stories about other people receiving all that they want. You've listed all that you want as though you already have it in your gratitude letter to the CSO, and you've anchored the good that's on its way to you into your subconscious through reading your letter out loud. The creative process is in motion.

The next step in the daily meeting with the CSO is the thinking part of the practice where you imagine what it's like to have the good that you've described. In this step, you see yourself in your mind's eye experiencing the good as yours. Some people call this imaging or visualization, and many have used it to gain greater success in their lives.

In her 2009 *Psychology Today* article "Seeing Is Believing: The Power of Visualization," Angie LeVan compiled a number of accounts from respected researchers and sports figures that describe how visualization has been used over the years: "Noted as one form of mental rehearsal, visualization has been popular since the Soviets started using it back in the 1970s to compete in sports. Now, many athletes employ this technique, including Tiger Woods, who has been using it since his preteen years. Seasoned athletes use vivid, highly detailed internal images and run-throughs of the entire performance, engaging all their senses in their mental rehearsal, and they combine their knowledge of the sports venue with mental rehearsal."

Jack Nicklaus, one of the greatest golfers in history, confirms the importance of visualization: "I never hit a shot, not even in practice, without having a very sharp, in-focus picture of it in my head. First I see the ball where I want it to finish, nice and white and sitting up high on the bright green grass. Then the scene quickly changes, and I see the ball going there: its path, trajectory, and shape, even its behavior on landing. Then there is a sort of fade-out, and the next scene shows me making the kind of swing that will turn the previous images into reality."

Boxer Muhammad Ali said about his career, "What keeps me going is goals." He consistently directed his thoughts, words, and emotions to confirm his goal: to be "the greatest." These sports figures have all been at the top of their game and exceptional.

You can use these same imaging techniques in this part of the meeting. Think about your gratitude statements and see yourself, in your mind, experiencing the good that you want. When you do, you'll be increasing your magnetism to draw what you want toward you. You'll also be preparing yourself to receive and keep the good that you want. Many of us can get things that we want, but to keep them requires preparation.

In 2008, the *Journal for the Society of Integrative Oncology* published a study that demonstrated that visualization reduced the reoccurrence of breast cancer. Involved in the study were thirty-four women who participated in an eight-week program that involved imagery. The study results found that the women who visualized good health had improved quality of life and reduced stress. It also recorded the cortisol rhythm, which is an indicator of the probability of the reoccurrence of cancer, was improved and the possibility of cancer returning was reduced. It is my belief that these women effectively used visualization to support their desire to maintain a cancer-free life.

As these examples demonstrate, when you see and feel yourself experiencing the good that you desire, you're preparing yourself mentally and physically to make that good permanently yours. This imaging process helps support the understanding that you deserve whatever you've claimed as yours. If you can see it, you can believe it.

Ask yourself questions as you picture having the good that you desire. See it in detail in your mind, just as Jack Nicklaus did. What does it feel and look like to reach your sales goals? How does it feel to have easy and professional relationships with coworkers and customers? What does that new office space look like, and how does it support you to become more profitable? How much joy and satisfaction will you have when your business expenses have been reduced? How much freedom will you experience when you have lots of money left in your bank account after paying all the bills? How great will it make you feel to bless others with gifts and other kindnesses?

In the CSO meeting, spend at least five minutes with your eyes closed after you've finished reading your gratitude letter and goals out loud and with emotion. Use this time to see and feel your good in your life now. How does your breathing and heartbeat change? Are you wearing a smile?

As I feel and imagine what it is like to experience the good that I am grateful for, I sit calmly with it and remain silent. In this quiet, I picture every detail that I can about the good that I want. I might see a sales report that shows that our company has met our goals. I might imagine myself receiving a signed contract for the amount I'd like and smiling ear to ear. I might imagine what it feels like to sit on a comfortable couch with my loved ones in my perfect home. I may watch the trees fly by as I ski down a powdery slope on a beautiful sunny day, laughing all the way. The more detail I can put into my vision and the more I can feel what it is like to experience the good that I want, the better.

Sometimes, while I'm imaging, I'll get a direction or lead on what I should do next toward receiving this good. These leads show up in lots of different ways. I might see a flash of someone to contact or something to do, a nudge or hunch to go somewhere, or an intuitive knowing that a course of action is required.

When you feel a nudge or hunch to take action or see a flash of someone to contact, know that this might be the CSO directing you through intuitive means. This unexpected message or feeling is the CSO's way of speaking to you. I noted a flash example earlier when I described receiving a mental image of a customer and then being guided to call her at her new health system. She subsequently placed a big order with my company.

Another example of a flash happened after I had been thanking the CSO in our meeting for feeling fulfilled as I helped others to grow and succeed. Within a week of using that gratitude statement, as I opened a door while leaving an event, my mind was filled with the face of a friend of mine. I knew that this flash was the direction from the CSO to call my friend. I contacted her later and learned she needed additional small group facilitators for a class she was teaching. I looked at my calendar, and, to my amazement, I had the time available to help her. Since performing that role, I have not only helped her serve her students in supportive ways but also experienced great joy and satisfaction as a manifestation of the good that I had been thanking the CSO for each morning.

Sometimes, this part of the practice may activate other visioning to occur. In one instance, my goal was to have a successful upcoming meeting with a large potential customer. I'd never met this customer before and imagined how the meeting might unfold. I imagined myself walking into the meeting, shaking hands, learning about the customer's needs, presenting solutions, and having a positive experience that resulted in an opportunity to submit a proposal. A few days before the meeting, I had a dream that was very similar to the imaging I had done. The only difference was that I could see the face of my potential customer in the dream. As I walked into the actual meeting, I literally met the man in my dream. I believe that my CSO enabled me to receive more information that might be helpful in achieving my goal. As it turned out, I felt comfortable in the meeting and achieved all my objectives as a first step toward signing a contract with this customer a few months later.

In the next chapter, we'll discuss in more detail the leads, hunches, nudges, flashes, and other intuitive directions that you'll receive from the CSO. If you don't get some lead or direction during your morning CSO meeting, don't be concerned. That's not the purpose of this part of the meeting, although it is sometimes an outcome. You're simply to think and imagine what the experience of having the good that you want would be like. The leads and directions will show up later and guide you to do what is next on the path toward your good.

Take comfort in knowing that the CSO is always working toward the good you've identified as yours. You've laid the groundwork by completing the CSO meeting for the day. That's all you need to do for now. Go ahead and adjourn the meeting and start the rest of your day. It's going to be a wonderful one as you and the CSO work together toward the good that you want.

There is a tremendous amount of good available to you, and you ought to have it. I am confident that your good is on its way to you now!

Exercise

Write down one of your gratitude statements from the CSO letter.

Thank you, CSO, for

_____ .

Now read it out loud with feeling. Next, close your eyes and imagine every detail of what it's like to experience that good. Use this time to see and feel the good in your life now. What are you doing as you experience this good? How do you feel? How do you look? What do your surroundings look like? Is there anyone with you? What's the lighting like? Where are you sitting, standing, moving? Are there any sounds? Imagine as many details as you can and feel the emotions that are being generated within you as you experience this good in your life.

As you open your eyes, notice how your body responds to this visualization of your goals. How do your breathing and heartbeat change? Are you wearing a smile?

Step 5

Expect Leads
and Follow Directions

*All our dreams can come true, if we have the courage
to pursue them.*

—Walt Disney

Congratulations! You've completed the CSO meeting and
have laid the groundwork for the creative process to produce
the results you desire. You may feel energized as you expect
a sign from the CSO directing you to take action toward
receiving what you desire. You don't have to try to make anything happen at this point. You're simply to watch for any
signs that could be providing you with the direction to take.

There is power in expecting results. Some of the best
brain research concerning expectations comes from Wol-
fram Schultz, a professor at Cambridge University. Schultz
has studied the relationship between dopamine and the
reward circuitry in the brain and found that positive expectations increase the levels of dopamine, which makes a

person more able to focus. The link between expectations, dopamine, and perception may explain why happiness is a great state for mental performance and problem solving. As mentioned earlier, Barbara Fredrickson from the University of North Carolina shows in her research that positive, happy people perceive a wider range of data, solve more problems, and come up with more ideas for action.

As I expect and watch for the leads and direction from the CSO, I have positive expectations and experience the same benefits that Shultz and Fredrickson have found in their studies. I am more able to focus, feel happier, and come up with more ideas for action. The only difference is that I believe the signs directing me to take action come from my partner the CSO and are specific to the good that I've proclaimed I want in my life.

The signs from the CSO may come to you in flashes (like the one that I described earlier, which directed me to contact my friend who needed a small group of facilitators). Or, you'll receive some other intuitive direction to take, such as a feeling or urge about something you heard, a friend you ran into, a location across town, a stranger passing by. Any of these could be the next step toward your good.

For example, I asked the CSO for a definite lead about whether to complete a contract with a San Diego company. Later, I drove by a sign that read, "May you celebrate your good fortune in San Diego." I knew in my gut that this was confirmation that I should agree to the business contract. A year after finalizing the contract, both the company and I had benefited financially from our relationship.

Flashes show up suddenly as a vision, thought, or idea. They seem to pop up out of nowhere without warning and have a strong mental impact. For me, a hunch is usually felt in the center of my body and brews there for a bit of time with emotion. As mentioned earlier, a flash or thought of my customer came to mind along with the hunch that I should call her. In following that direction from the CSO, I received the $400,000 in sales for our business that I had previously proclaimed as the good that I wanted.

Another time, I woke up in the middle of the night from a sound sleep with the thought of my sister and that I should call her. As you can imagine, I had to think twice about calling her home at three o'clock in the morning, knowing that I would wake up her entire household. But I've learned to follow the directions from the CSO, so I called. She was awake with an awful sickness and wanted some comfort and prayerful support to proclaim perfect health for her. We recited affirmative statements about her perfect, whole, and complete health until she felt better and could return to sleep. The next morning, she felt well enough to go to work.

The good for me in this situation was consistent with the gratitude I regularly proclaimed in the CSO meeting for harmonious and supportive relationships with all my family members. I got to experience love and healing support operating through me while on the phone with my sister, and in return I felt loved and supported as well and slept great after the call. I didn't feel the least bit tired the next morning.

Action Faith

When you get flashes or hunches, don't question them— just do what you feel led to do by the CSO. This shows action faith! I use the term "action faith" deliberately to remind you that action must be taken when you receive a lead. I want you to fully recognize that taking action is a necessary step to receiving the good that you want. Ernest Holmes, the founder of Religious Science as part of the greater New Thought movement, writes, "A faith without works is merely a belief in a theory that you have not proved to be true. Active faith [or action faith in my terms] is the knowing, by experience, that your theory can be proved." Action faith is very important to proving the value of your partnership with the CSO.

If for some reason you don't understand the intuitive lead or directive, ask the CSO for a confirming sign to gain some clarity. As a response, you may get another flash or hunch. You may receive an intuitive message through a gut feeling to do something or go somewhere. You may feel something intense when a word is spoken by a friend or a stranger. If you're consistent with your practice, you'll get better at recognizing when something is a response to your request for a lead.

For example, my friend had thanked the CSO for a successful investment strategy for retirement during her daily practice. She hadn't started a retirement plan yet, but she desired a successful plan and thanked the CSO for it as though it had already manifested. She started to notice unsolicited emails advertising companies that could help with investment strategies. She wasn't sure if she was supposed to contact these companies, so she asked the CSO for another lead. Within two days of asking for the lead, a woman she knew came to mind in a flash and my friend felt a hunch to call her. She didn't know why, but she called the woman anyway. In their discussion, she learned that this woman had just started an investment group with other experienced and successful women. The intention was to successfully plan for the group members' retirements. My friend was elated and told the woman what she had been wanting. As a result, my friend was asked to join the group. Some months later, she had in place a strong plan for her retirement. She has also made new friends and learned a tremendous amount from these successful businesswomen in the process. The CSO directed her to receive her desired good and more!

Flashes, hunches, and nudges are all intuitive leads. My friend followed the lead to call her friend even though she didn't know the reason or outcome for making the call. This is the part of the practice that takes courage. Most successful businesspeople agree that following intuitive messages is an important element to achieving their goals. Bill Gates said, "Often you have to rely on intuition." And Steve Jobs agreed when he advised us to "have the courage to follow your heart and intuition." The CSO wants us to be successful, and it will always do its part to give us leads to take the next step toward our good. Our part is to take action.

Following the directions that you get from the CSO as intuitive leads can be one of the most difficult parts of this practice. Often, we want to know and understand the reason for the CSO's direction. We want it to be logical. We want to know what the outcome of a particular course of action is going to be before we commit. We question the direction because it doesn't make sense to us at the time. But a central component to the success of this seven-step path is learning to trust those intuitive moments.

When you get a lead, hunch, flash, or intuitive direction, just do it, knowing that the CSO is working through this action for your good. Proclaim out loud that there are no mistakes in the CSO as the all-knowing power of the universe. This does not mean, however, that you should take action without getting a lead first. That kind of behavior can take you in a completely different direction, away from your good, making the journey to your good longer and harder as a result.

Throwing a Fleece

If a lead or direction makes you feel unsure or uncomfortable, go ahead and ask the CSO for another lead. It doesn't mind being questioned; in fact, it wants you to be as certain as possible that your good is on the way. I call this "throwing a fleece."

Gideon, one of my favorite characters in the Bible, was the youngest son in his family and had very low self-esteem. The story states that an angel of God informed Gideon that he had been chosen to lead the army of Israel to victory. Gideon didn't believe that this direction was really from God and told the angel that he must be mistaken. The angel of God insisted that Gideon was the chosen one. To confirm that this was true, Gideon asked for signs to prove it. Well, Gideon got some pretty big signs, but he was still unsure about whether God meant that he was the chosen one to lead the army of Israel. So, to confirm this beyond a doubt, the story says that Gideon employed fleeces from sheep for a series of tests.

One night, Gideon asked that the ground be wet with dew and the fleece on top of the ground remain dry. No problem. When Gideon checked the next day, it was exactly as he'd prescribed. Gideon still wasn't convinced, so he asked for the opposite sign. The second night, the ground was to remain dry and the fleece was to be wet. Again, God provided these signs to Gideon. He became confident that it was God giving him direction. As a result of the leads and signs, he moved forward with God to complete his mission successfully.

The point of this story isn't in its literal interpretation. It is an illustration showing that it's normal to have doubts about directions that at first don't make sense to you. It's fine to ask for signs, confirmation, or another lead. As Gideon got his signs, so will you.

"Throwing a fleece" or "pulling a Gideon" has now become the way I describe asking for additional clarification, confirmation, and more leads to ensure that I understand the direction the CSO wants me to go in or the action I am to take.

Once you've asked for a sign and received a response, be sure to follow the direction so that you can get one step closer to realizing your good. If you're still uncomfortable with the direction you've been given, you can start walking the way of the direction and proclaiming out loud, "CSO, I feel that this is the direction that you're leading me in. If this is not the right path, block it and redirect my course. If this is the right path, make my way clear."

Doing this is an example of taking an action or showing action faith. You're taking an active step toward your good as you feel guided by the CSO while still asking for confirming direction. As you repeatedly follow the guidance you receive, future leads will become easier to notice and your confidence will grow.

Sometimes you may get a lead or flash to contact someone that you haven't thought of or spoken to in a very long time. You may even feel apprehensive or uncomfortable about making the call because your last encounter with the person was unpleasant. Go ahead and "throw a fleece." Ask for another unmistakable lead.

A student of mine met with her CSO daily and claimed peace, love, and freedom as part of the good she wanted to receive. At the end of the first week, she had a flash about a woman she had worked with years before. She actually hated this woman, who had treated her horribly and done unforgivable things. My student tried to disregard the flashes, but at all hours of the day, she would have thoughts of this woman with a hunch to call her. She did not want to contact or forgive this woman and asked for other leads to get to the good that she wanted, but the flashes and thoughts of the woman continued. After four weeks of what she referred to as turmoil, she made the call. She learned that the woman was in the hospital with a short time to live. The woman asked my student to forgive her and expressed how sorry she was for all that had gone on in the past. A week after the call, the woman died.

My student didn't necessarily need the woman to ask for forgiveness and say she was sorry in order to become free. But, as it turned out, it helped her immensely. She felt more peace, love, and freedom as a result of the experience. She also discovered some compassion for the dying woman, who admitted that she wished she would have lived her life differently. I'm always amazed at how the CSO knows exactly the right path for us to take in order to experience the highest and best good that we want.

As you consistently use this part of the practice, it will become easier to notice and follow the leads from the CSO. If you've ever heard the phone ring and known intuitively who was calling before you answered, then you can understand what I am saying about this. When intuitive messages, leads, and hunches come to you, you'll recognize which are from the CSO and which are not. Your trust in the CSO, as you build on your ongoing relationship, will enable you to know intuitively when you are being called to do something. The CSO wants to direct your steps toward your good. Your courage, trust, and action faith will ensure that you make progress toward receiving everything that is in your best interest.

Exercise

After at least three days of your daily CSO meeting and following your agenda, write down one of your gratitude statements for the good that you want.

Thank you, CSO, for

- *my healthy, vital, strong body*
- *for the lovely trip to Ld's*
- *Thank you for my 15th Ø party.*

What flashes, hunches, intuitive nudges, or unexplained messages have you noticed? Write down the one that stands out for you below.

missing Patty, she called.
for Carol's + Marilyn's
pep insightful talk about
my feelings of dependency
how my mother made me wary
about trying new things

stepping out on my own
Remember the strong Ø that jumped!

What action faith have you taken (or could you take now) that doesn't make you feel uncomfortable or at risk?

_____

_____

If you don't feel comfortable with trying action faith just yet, write a request for another lead below:

_____

_____

Step 6

Celebrate and Note Demonstrations

The more you praise and celebrate your life, the more there is in life to celebrate.

—Oprah Winfrey

By this point in the practice, you'll have had a chance to show action faith and take some of the steps toward your good as directed by the CSO. You may have already achieved the good that you want or experienced some successful progress. Now it's time to celebrate!

Celebrating is not only fun, it also reinforces in your mind that the CSO practice is something you want to continue. The more you celebrate, the more you will want to find reasons to celebrate.

In his book *The Brain That Changes Itself*, Dr. Norman Doidge says that the brain has the capacity to rewire itself and/or form new neural pathways. Getting up in the morning for the CSO meeting, performing a daily spiritual routine, and celebrating when some good shows up are the kinds of actions that benefit from repetition, which reinforces new learning.

Once a demonstration of any good shows up, express gratitude in a joyful way. High-five a colleague, jump up and down with a friend and cheer for joy, or call a family member to celebrate on the phone. It may sound nonessential, but this is an important part of the practice. It supports expectancy and changes your energy level to one that's best for attracting more good.

If you know that you will get to celebrate when anything good shows up, and celebrating is joyful and fun, you're engaging your emotions to attract more of your good. You are acting as a magnet for it. Celebration is a really wonderful part of the practice.

When we received a request for a proposal to work with a large, prestigious hospital system, my business partner and I jumped up and down with gratitude. We hadn't considered that our small company would have the opportunity to pitch ourselves as a vendor for this particular customer. We enthusiastically celebrated this turn of events and were excited to prepare our response.

During the preparation of our response, we learned that at least four other companies had been invited to submit proposals, all of them much larger than we were. We heard a rumor from an industry colleague that one of the competitors planned to bid $1 million less than we would. These situations could have swayed our conviction and instilled fear in us, but it didn't. I knew that my company couldn't match the lower pricing and still make a profit, so I didn't focus on that. Instead, I focused on feeling grateful that we were being considered as a possible vendor at all. We did the best job that we could to prepare a fair response that highlighted the value we could offer.

In my daily CSO meetings, I began to say out loud, as though it had happened already, "Thank you, CSO, that this customer chooses our company as their supplier if we are the best solution that meets their needs. Thank you that we all work harmoniously together and appreciate any new partnership that may develop. Thank you that we easily meet our sales goals for the year with the right customers, giving perfect satisfaction."

These gratitude statements described the good that I wanted. I didn't spend time focusing on what I didn't want or what could have made me fearful. Instead, I proclaimed that I was grateful my company was meeting our sales goals with the right customers in whatever way was best.

As it turned out, my company was awarded the $3 million contract, which led to a close and harmonious relationship with all of the customer representatives for many years. As you can imagine, my business partner and I jumped up and down shouting with joy and gratitude again when we were notified that we were the chosen supplier. And our company easily and joyfully exceeded all our sales goals that year as well.

I can't confirm what our competitors bid for the project, but it didn't matter. I didn't put any energy or thought toward wanting my competitors to lose the business. It is never the trait of a successful person to want another's failure.

I like how Zig Ziglar puts it: "Life is an echo. What you send out comes back. What you sow, you reap. What you give, you get. What you see in others exists in you." I agree. If you send any negative energy to others, you're attracting the same to yourself. You'll believe this more fully as you continue to spend time partnering with the CSO to achieve your goals. You'll recognize that the all-knowing universal power is unlimited and that everyone, including competitors, can receive the good things that they desire without affecting the amount of good that you receive.

When something good shows up, celebrate with someone you trust—in person, by phone, or even online—so that you can remain magnetic to your good. If you don't have anyone immediately available, request to join our Facebook group page at www.facebook.com/groups/CSOPracticeAlumni/ by sending an email request to csogroup@bizzultz.com. You can post your demonstrations there, and I promise I will virtually jump up and down with you, saying, "Yay for you and your good!"

After celebrating, take the time to write down your demonstrations of good. Carry a separate notebook or an electronic notepad for the purpose of writing down your demonstrations throughout the day. This has a powerful effect, as we discussed earlier. A written record of the demonstrations you've achieved acts as proof that you can refer back to at a later time. Each step you take that gets you closer to your good is a cause for celebration. All leads that you've received from the CSO are worth recording. Your good is on its way!

You can think of a demonstration of the CSO working in your favor like this: birds fly around a boat on the ocean before anyone can see land, but the birds indicate that land is close. Some demonstrations are like the seabirds—signs that the good that you want is close. I've had this happen many times.

Several years ago, prior to the CSO practice, I wanted a new, more professional wardrobe than the one I had. I used the affirmative prayer techniques I knew at that time and was grateful in advance for these new clothes. I imagined what they'd look like and how powerful and successful I would feel when I walked into business meetings wearing them.

A friend of mine heard about my desire and gave me a beautiful dress coat made in London that she never wore. I knew this was a sign my new wardrobe was on its way. The coat was like the birds flying from land before it appeared. It prepared me to receive the gift of my new wardrobe. I wrote down this demonstration and celebrated by calling my best friend. About a month later, I was given $2,500 through my company for an error in sales commission calculations. Our finance manager had missed paying a bonus six months earlier. I bought beautiful new clothes with the bonus and was grateful.

When recording your demonstrations, nothing is too small to consider as a sign that the CSO is directing you toward your good. As you look back on demonstrations you've written down, you will build your confidence and trust that more good is on the way.

Sometimes our emotions or energy levels are not as balanced as we'd like, and we feel tired and run down. This is an excellent time to pull out your notes about demonstrations that you've received, review them, and trust that what the CSO had done before the CSO now does again. Your demonstration log is the proof.

Exercise

Identify at least two friends, family members, or colleagues that you talk with often and with whom you have a supportive relationship. Let each of them know that you'd like to begin celebrating success as part of a prosperity practice. Tell them that you'd like to celebrate with them right away when something good happens to either of you or when you've achieved your goals. Suggest that each of you text, email, or leave a message with the word "Hooray!" to the other as an indicator that it's time to celebrate, and make a date shortly after that to tell the story and celebrate. Write down your demonstrations so that you can refer back to them to continue to build your confidence that the CSO will always direct you to your good.

Step 7

End Your Day with Gratitude and Forgiveness

*We must develop and maintain the capacity to forgive.
He who is devoid of the power to forgive is devoid of
the power to love.*

—Martin Luther King Jr.

You've now made it to the final step in your new daily practice. Take a moment to congratulate yourself on a terrific day partnering with the CSO. You've laid the foundation to experience more of the good that you desire, and you have a deeper understanding of your and the CSO's clear and separate responsibilities in the partnership.

You have fulfilled your part by claiming what you want as your good, thanking the CSO for that good in writing and speaking with emotion, and imagining the good as you will experience it in your life. The CSO has created paths to your good and provided you with leads to follow to get there, and in turn you have followed the guidance to move

g the path to your good and celebrated your achievement.

You've had a busy day! Now there is just one more step before you drift off to sleep. You have an additional responsibility that enables you to receive your good without delay.

Once you're finished preparing for bed, you'll need to be in a place where you can speak out loud. If you're concerned about privacy or not interrupting your partner's sleep, go to the quiet area where you hold the CSO morning meeting to do this final step.

Start by thanking the CSO for a great day and for all the good you've received, including the marvelous people who are in your life. If challenges presented themselves, thank the CSO for handling the situations for your highest and best good and for the good of any others who are involved.

My summary might include the following: "CSO, thank you for a great day. I sincerely appreciate the people I work with, my clients, my suppliers, my friends, and my family. I appreciate the new customer contract that we received today and the discount that I got on my car service. Thank you for our customer Fred, who realizes that we're there to support him and his staff. Thank you for seeing that any challenges that may be occurring in his operations are dissolved and replaced by great and flawless service for Fred and his team. For all your guidance that led me to the good that I desire, I thank you."

Right after the gratitude summary, the final part of your day is to speak the following with sincerity:

> CSO, if there is anyone from my past or present that I need to forgive, whether I remember them or not, I now do so. I bless them, I love them, I forgive them, and I release them into your care, knowing that you will work with them in whatever way is best. And if there is anyone from my past or present who needs to forgive me, including myself, they now do so, and we are all free to experience a higher and greater good in our lives.
> (grace)

How do you feel after reading the forgiveness part of the practice out loud? You may be thinking that you don't feel much forgiveness or even that you don't want to forgive everyone from your past or present. A few people may have come to mind that you'd like to exclude from this part of the practice entirely. This is a normal feeling, but please don't exclude anyone.

Forgiveness doesn't mean that you absolve a person for their actions, or place yourself in a position to be hurt by them again. Forgiveness means that you can recognize they did something wrong, but you can also choose to not let them or the situation have power over you anymore. You can choose to let it go and become free. You can choose to be powerful and create a wonderful future for yourself. Forgiveness is a necessary part of making this choice. With forgiveness, you are making room for the CSO to work and creating the calm place to receive the direction toward the good that you want, even if you don't necessarily feel like forgiving today. Forgiveness is for your benefit, not anyone else's.

You can also think about it this way: Anything that may be blocking the communication channel between you and your CSO needs to be removed so that you can recognize the intuitive leads that are being sent to you. If your thoughts are consumed with resentment, it becomes harder for the CSO's messages to get through to direct you toward your goals. There is a great spiritual axiom that states, "Whatever you hold against another you also hold against yourself." By letting go of these resentments, you free up your energy to receive more of the good you deserve. A great way to do this is by saying the forgiveness prayer each night.

You don't have to feel that the words are true or even that you want to forgive everyone at this point. Just say the words each night with as much sincerity as you can muster, and include everyone. This is part of the practice. Although it may be tough, it will pay off for you in the end. It will also get easier over time.

I can tell you from experience that you will gain lasting freedom as you apply techniques of forgiveness. In this freedom, you will create a place for the good that you want. You'll also find over time that these techniques become easier to use and there will be fewer reasons for you to use them. Many of my students have told me that the forgiveness practice has brought about the most revelations. You may find that someone you hadn't thought of in years somehow comes to mind after using this part of the practice. This may be a lead that you need to do some forgiveness work. Doing the work willingly will open channels for you to receive more of the good that you want sooner.

One student commented that someone whom she had forgotten and held some unforgiving thoughts toward suddenly contacted her after fifteen years to congratulate her on an award she received. Only when he contacted her did my student recognize that she still had a grudge against him for causing an expensive business problem and not taking responsibility for it. She realized that she needed to work on forgiving him because the thought of him made her tense.

She began to use techniques for forgiveness toward the man and herself. I gave her an easy-to-remember mantra that I had heard long before: "I bless you, I love you, I forgive you, I release you." She was to recite this mantra out loud every time she thought of this man.

She didn't feel any peace right away, and she couldn't say that she forgave him, either. But she persisted. She continued to recite the mantra whenever she thought of him and felt tension in her body. By the end of the first week, she felt a little lighter and freer while she said the forgiveness mantra. By the following week, the words began to have a new meaning for her and she actually started to believe them. After two weeks of saying the forgiveness mantra, she realized that she had developed some compassion for the man. She realized that he had made poor life choices and was working to make amends. That's why he had ccontacted her. That took courage.

By the third week, when she felt more peace about this person, a company that had discontinued carrying her product line the previous year called unexpectedly and renewed a contract with her company. She received several thousand dollars in new orders as a result. Might that have happened anyway? Sure, since she was also doing the rest of her daily practice. But, due to forgiveness, she may have welcomed her good to arrive sooner. She made room in her life to receive more good without further delay.

You can do this, too, and not only develop a life that is freer and filled with your good but also healthier. In 2006, Dr. Fred Luskin, author of *Forgive for Good*, and other researchers set out to determine whether people diagnosed with stage 1 hypertension could lower their blood pressure after going through a program that taught them how to forgive. Anger expression and blood pressure were measured to determine the effects. After eight weeks of using the forgiveness practice, the study showed a significant reduction in the blood pressure of the subjects. Researchers believe that this kind of forgiveness training may be effective for some patients who have high levels of anger combined with hypertension. Dr. Luskin also created the Stanford University Forgiveness Project. "The results were very positive," he said. "People showed less stress, less anger, more optimism and more forgiveness."

In the study "Neuroimaging of Forgivability," Dr. Tom Farrow, a clinical psychologist at the University of Sheffield, and his colleagues used magnetic resonance imaging (MRI) to study the effects of forgiveness on the brain. When a person is in the process of forgiving, the scanned images show that activity in the frontal lobe of the brain increases. The frontal lobe is involved in problem solving, complex thought, and the complex functions of thinking and reasoning. Based on this research, is it possible that forgiving someone may actually make you smarter? Or help you make better business and financial decisions?

In addition to the health and intelligence benefits of forgiveness, this part of the practice is another stepping-stone on the path of understanding how to have a deeper and more fulfilling relationship with the CSO and others. As we forgive, we experience a new sense of freedom and peace. We can see more possibilities in our business and beyond. The only way to learn this, however, is to use the practice.

I saw a speaker demonstrate how forgiveness frees us by asking a man from the audience to come on stage. He tied one end of a rope to the man's ankle and attached the other end to his own ankle. He made up a story saying that the man had done something awful to him long ago and the last person he wanted to see was this man. But whenever he thought of the man, it was like being tied to him. His emotions were that strong and negative. It was as if he deliberately kept the man nearby and attached to him through the power of his negative emotions.

The speaker went on to explain that the only way for him to be truly free from the man was to untie the rope through forgiveness. The ultimate goal, he said, was to get to a point where any thoughts of the person would no longer evoke an emotional reaction. The key in the message is the realization that you and I have the power to untie the rope and gain freedom, and no one can do it for us.

Remember, you have power over your own life, not anyone else. I encourage you to use these tools to build a life free from anything binding you to painful past experiences. The CSO as the universal power wants you to receive your good and needs your help. By forgiving people from your past and letting go of any feelings of resentment and anger you free up the room to receive the good things that the CSO has in store for you.

Sometimes the person we most need to forgive is ourselves. You may be critical of yourself for something you did in the past. The same daily practice and forgiveness prayers can be used to gain a deeper sense of peace and freedom about yourself. The CSO can help you to recognize how any mistakes you made in the past were a necessary part of growing toward your good.

Even if the results aren't obvious when you start the forgiveness practice and mantras, be persistent. Eventually some bit of good will shine through. Use this newfound demonstration to build your confidence and transform the situation.

I have been critical of myself for what I felt were past mistakes. I spent a lot of time using the forgiveness mantras and thanking the CSO for turning these situations into something good. I used my daily spiritual practice to proclaim a new truth about those past mistakes: "Thank you, CSO, for allowing me to look in the rearview mirror of life and see how my past and any decisions I made were necessary for the good that I am experiencing now and always."

It's sometimes taken several years after an event that left me feeling critical of myself to be able to see how that painful experience has turned into positivity through forgiveness work and the power of the CSO. For example, I once experienced tremendous difficulty and pain after deciding to leave a company that I started. Three years later, after using the forgiveness practice, I saw how that decision had provided the money and time to start a new company that was even more successful. When you look deeper at any situation, you will ultimately see it as a necessary part of the journey to receive your good.

Exercise

Copy the forgiveness part of the practice onto a separate piece of paper and put it where you'll do the evening part of the practice. When it is time to go to bed, think of someone whom you're having trouble forgiving. As you think of that person or anyone else that you have anger or resentment toward, say the forgiveness statement out loud, or the simpler, "I bless you, I love you, I forgive you, I release you."

What good do you want most in your life? Create a gratitude statement as though you've already received this good and state it right after the forgiveness mantra above.

Transfer the forgiveness mantra and gratitude statement to a card that you can put in your wallet. Write, "I bless you, I love you, I forgive you, I release you." Below that, write your gratitude statement, "Thank you, CSO, for _____
_____."

Each time the person whom you hold anger or resentment toward comes to mind, pull out the card and read the forgiveness mantra and gratitude statement a minimum of five times.

As your good manifests, update your gratitude statement to receive higher and greater good.

As we come to the end of your introduction to the seven steps, it's important to remember that your relationship and partnership with the CSO is your own. After practicing all the daily CSO steps for a minimum of thirty days, you will be divinely inspired and gain confidence to realize more of the things that you want than ever before. You will continue to grow in your unique and wonderful relationship with the CSO, your partner in business and in life.

There is a tremendous amount of good ready and waiting for you, and you will have it!

In part two of this book we will delve deeper into the practice to help you troubleshoot any blocks or difficulties that may come up along the way.

Going Deeper with the Seven-Step Practice

When you are grateful, fear disappears and abundance appears.

—Anthony Robbins

Now that you have a daily practice, you should be seeing some benefits in aligning yourself with the CSO as your partner. You may be feeling lighter and more energetic. You may be receiving messages and directions. As you become more focused on what you want and give gratitude for it daily, the CSO should be giving you leads for the how, or steps that you're to take to get to your good. Here are a few of the stories I've received from students using the CSO practice.

In the past week, I affirmed and thanked the CSO for increased sales in our business. Within two days of starting the daily practice, I was told by my credit manager that we had a $15 credit on the books for one of our customers. Two days later, I felt a hunch to contact the local buyer for the customer to let her know about this credit. This didn't make logical sense since we'd normally just apply the credit to the next invoice. But I did what I felt I was being intuitively led to do and made the call without question.

When I did, the buyer answered and put me on speaker-phone to introduce me to the head of purchasing for all their stores across the United States. The head of purchasing was in town only for the day. In our phone discussion, she said that she had seen our products at their local store and asked me several more questions about my company. The head of purchasing confirmed our sales performance figures with the local buyer and then told me that she planned to carry some of our products in more of their stores nationwide. This will prove to be one of our largest orders ever. Thank you, CSO.

I run a department in an office in Seattle. I had been having some trouble over the prior couple of months with an employee who clearly wasn't happy with her job. We had a strained relationship, and I was never sure what kind of mood she'd be in day to day. I felt nervous and worried that I was going to end up letting her go if she continued to be a problem and that this would adversely affect the other employees in the office. I started to use the daily CSO practice and included the affirmation, "Only those employees that are for our highest and best good work for us. All others find their good elsewhere." I said this dozens of times each day.

After a few days, I started to feel less nervous when I thought of my employee. By the end of the second week of following the steps in the practice, the problem employee asked to meet with me and submitted her resignation. She apologized for being so irritable over the past couple of months and explained that she had been anxious about an important decision that she had to make. She'd decided to get married and move to Florida. I'm so grateful that I didn't have to be the one to let her go and that she is able to receive her good and happiness elsewhere. Thanks, CSO.

I had been out of work for over six months and had sent out dozens of résumés to find a new position. I wasn't called back for any interviews. I was discouraged and worried about how I would survive without a job. I began to use the daily practice and thanked the CSO for the perfect job. I admit that I wasn't sure how this was going to help me. I just kept doing the practice and following the daily steps. On the fourth day, I felt some guidance as a nudge to revise my résumé. The thought and words came to mind and settled there. Normally, I would have just let the thoughts go, but the daily practice made me pay attention and ask, "Could this be the CSO?" I wasn't sure, but I went ahead and rewrote my résumé with what I felt guided to write about myself.

I responded the next day to three job advertisements using my new résumé and was called over the following few days for three interviews. I was amazed since there had been no interview activity for several months prior to the lead that I got to revise my résumé. I went to all of the interviews this past week and felt very confident in the meetings. Two of the three companies have now offered me jobs, and I expect that the third company will also. Wow, what a pleasure and delight it is to be able to choose how best to use my talents. I'm a huge believer in the power of partnering with the CSO.

What you may be recognizing by now is that this practice calls you to use less of your effort to make things happen. This can be tough, since many of us have developed the habit to micromanage our lives. We want to know the future. But it's when we surrender the design of the path over to the CSO that we experience the maximum good in the least amount of time.

Some of my students have admitted that they like to be in control and giving that up is difficult for them. They're used to doing everything and making things happen. Many of us want to know the outcome before taking a step or making a decision. My advice to you is to persist with attending the daily CSO meeting and intend with conviction that you will be able to follow all of the steps each day. Your job is to establish the "what" that you want. The job of the CSO is to establish the path to get there, or the "how," and give you directions. You have to commit to letting the CSO do its job and trust that it can perform better than you think is possible. As you continue in the practice, it will get easier.

Although I've worked for several years to prove that this daily CSO practice is effective in achieving goals, I recognize that it's possible that you may not get the leads that you want as quickly as you'd like. Sometimes students will tell me that they are doing all the steps in the practice but are not getting any closer to the good they want. This may be a true statement for them. I have experienced the same thing in the past.

Sometimes our good can be delayed when old beliefs and habits are operating through us without our recognizing them consciously. This isn't uncommon. It is one of the main reasons I ask that the daily practice be followed for a minimum of thirty days. During that time, you're actually retraining yourself. You're working to establish new beliefs and habits that will support you in receiving the things you want, rather than focusing on things you don't want.

In the following chapters, I'm going to provide additional information that may be helpful when you feel stuck or aren't getting clear directions. Applying this information to your daily practice will help you become a more effective partner to the CSO and further facilitate the good that you want into your life.

This is an exciting time as you deepen your understanding of success principles to receive an even greater and higher good in your life.

Exercise

After reading the success stories of students using the CSO daily practice, what do you remember as key points? Did you identify with any situations? Why?

After attending at least seven CSO meetings, describe your experience. List any leads from the CSO that you have received.

Words, Thoughts, and Emotions as Tools

You can change your world by changing your words. Remember, death and life are in the power of the tongue.

—Joel Osteen

Many people don't comprehend the power of their words, thoughts, and emotions. When we understand fully just how powerful these are, we carefully choose what to say, think, and feel. The spoken word plays a central role in our lives.

People are often surprised when they realize that they get what they've given voice to. Many of us have spoken about things we don't want in our lives or used our words to confirm our unfortunate position in life. And since that is what we have given our voice to, we receive more of the same.

For example, my friend Sam had a sales job with a large corporation. In spite of meeting all of his goals and quotas, he felt that his boss wasn't treating him fairly. As Sam focused on and spoke about not being treated fairly by his boss, more and more things would happen to demonstrate that he was treated unfairly. He'd say things like, "I know my boss doesn't like me and is doing things that will make me fail." Consistent with his fears, Sam's sales commissions were reduced. He would say, "My boss is single and jealous of me and my family. I know he's going to do something to disrupt my home life." Within a month of repeating this fear in increasing amounts, Sam's job schedule changed so that he had to spend more time traveling and away from his family. The words that Sam spoke, charged with the fearful emotions he felt, attracted the outcome that he received. Eventually, Sam was filled with all-consuming fear. He started to voice his fear of losing his job. As you might expect, he was laid off a short time later.

How often has this kind of thing happened to you? How often have you allowed the feelings of fear and anxiety to be all consuming? How often have you used phases like, "I hope my schedule doesn't change," "I hope my hours don't get reduced," or "I'm so upset my boss/coworker is treating me so poorly"? What did you get as a result of this? If you use the power of your words in this way, you often get more of what you *don't* want, because you have used your words, thoughts, and emotions to proclaim and attract exactly that.

The key to changing this is to choose words, thoughts, and emotions that support what you *do* want, not what you don't. In the case of Sam, he recognized after meeting with me that his words, thoughts, and emotions supported his fears and played a leading part in his losing his job. I assured him that not only could he make a choice to use his words for his good, he could also use his words to allow the all-knowing universal power to transform any past mistakes. Somehow, the situation of being laid off could work in his favor.

At first, Sam didn't believe this was possible. But he made the commitment to change his words. Together we created statements for him to say out loud that would support receiving his good: "I am grateful that I now have the perfect job that is fun, easy, satisfying, and fulfilling. I have great relationships with all my coworkers and customers. I make more money than I ever have before, and all related to me and my work are happy by it."

For the first few days, Sam did not believe these affirmative gratitude statements. His thoughts were filled with fear and appeared out of control. The fearful recording going round and round in his mind included thoughts about how awful it would be to not get a job and be able to support his family. He wondered if his old boss was bad-mouthing him in the industry so that no other companies would want to hire him. When Sam shared these thoughts with me, I told him that this was normal for most people and to try not to beat himself up about it. All that was happening was that his fears were distracting him and trying to hold him hostage. To become free and get what he wanted, which was a good-paying job that was satisfying and fun, he needed to use his words to overpower the negative and fearful thoughts. He needed to see this as a personal competition for his attention. He could decide which side would win out.

Sam used to be a football player in high school and knew about overpowering the competition. He knew that practicing a lot and being more prepared than the competition would help win the game. Sam remembered what it felt like to practice with determination. Stating affirmative words over and over became part of his preparation and practice to overpower fear.

I also told Sam that it was equally important to send words and thoughts of forgiveness to his former boss so that his emotional condition could become calm and give the all-knowing universal power the opportunity to work. This forgiveness work would ensure that there was perfect weather to play so he could win the game! Sam didn't like that much, but he committed to doing the forgiveness work in order to win.

Over the following two weeks, Sam was diligent about using the daily affirmative statements and forgiveness mantras every time a negative thought about his former boss or his situation came to mind. He also met with me as his supportive friend. He did everything necessary to demolish any negative thoughts and doubts that rose up.

During the third week of consistent practice, Sam received a job offer from a large company without having to apply for the position or prepare a revised résumé. The offer included a raise of more than 15 percent over what he made at his previous job, and he didn't have to pack up his family and move. A valued customer whom he was friendly with had told the company that Sam was an excellent salesperson and available for hire. The valued customer went on to say that he liked working with Sam and would do so again.

Not only did Sam receive a better job, but he could also look at the situation of being laid off as something that the all-knowing universal power used for his good. If he hadn't been laid off he wouldn't have gotten the better job. He was actually able to feel gratitude when sending thoughts of forgiveness to his previous boss. How wonderful! The CSO turned what seemed like a bad situation at the time into Sam's good.

If you are in a situation where you feel hurt by the actions of another or you feel that someone had a hand in "ruining your life," know that the CSO can turn any past wrongdoing into your good. Start using your words, thoughts, and emotions now to proclaim this truth: "Any hurtful situations or seeming mistakes of my past are now turned into something positive. In the rearview mirror of life, I will be able to look back and see how all situations helped me to receive my heart's desires with grace and in perfect ways."

Sam now has the tools to implement a daily practice to go from good to greater good in his work and his life. "My CSO is so good," is one of Sam's favorite sayings today.

Word choices and sentence structures are vital to your success. When I speak with gratitude and confidence about what I want, I usually get more of it. When I speak with fear or worry about what I don't want, I also get more of that. Your life today is a reflection of the words you are speaking, the thoughts you are thinking, and the emotions you are feeling.

According to Lissa Rankin, MD, author of *Mind Over Medicine*, a study of medical students showed that 79 percent of them develop symptoms similar to the illnesses they are studying. They focus so much attention on the symptoms that they began to manifest them within themselves. Dr. Rankin goes on to say, "You wouldn't take a pill from a bottle with a skull and crossbones on it, but every time you think negative thoughts about your health, you're potentially poisoning your body with stress hormones that deactivate your body's natural self-repair mechanisms." Dr. Rankin supports the idea that you can heal yourself with your thoughts and words, but you can also make yourself sick as well if you're focusing on what you don't want to happen.

Take great care to choose the speech, thoughts, and emotions that are consistent with the life that you want. This is sometimes easier to say than do, especially since many of us have been trained to focus on the problem in an attempt to fix it.

At the company I started when I was nineteen, I hired an employee whose behavior would often upset other employees and customers. I would pray in the fashion that I had been taught: "God, please keep this employee from doing so much harm," or something along the lines of "praying the problem." I used reactive prayer to petition God for help when I was in trouble. I didn't know that I should focus on what I wanted and hadn't fully mastered how to use affirmative gratitude statements.

As I pleaded with God to keep the employee from doing more harm, all that got me was an employee continuing to do harm. All of my words, thoughts, and emotions focused on the employee causing harm, and that was what

I received. It was exhausting. I now know that it would have been better to use a gratitude statement process instead: "God, thank you that only those people who are for our highest and best good now work for us. All others find their good elsewhere."

As it turned out, the problem employee left our company after I began to envision her as gone and happy in a new job. I told my business partner that I wanted the employee to quit so that she could have a job doing something she liked better in a different company. I forced myself to imagine how happy she would be to get her ideal job and the freedom I would then experience. I saw both of us as very happy. Within a month, the employee informed me that she had received a better job offer with another company. I jumped up and down with her, celebrating her good fortune (and mine). More than thirty years later, I recognize that the process of visioning that I used at nineteen was a more advanced practice that allowed my problem employee and me to both receive what we wanted.

In my most recent business, I used the affirmative gratitude statement method as I partnered with the CSO to attract employees. My job in the CSO partnership was to claim that I wanted the right employees to work for us. The CSO's responsibility was to enable those employees to be found by me and to prevent any employees that weren't right for our company from showing up.

It worked! Our business assembled an incredibly talented and diverse team of employees. Everyone worked well together; they loved their jobs and valued their work. They felt that they were appreciated, and many of their ideas for improvements were implemented. Even though their jobs required them to work longer hours than many of their peers in other companies, they appreciated feeling empowered. What I witnessed, and what customers told me they saw, indicated that our employees were living this attitude of being valued and appreciated. The words they said to me were made manifest.

To go from good to greater good, use supportive words and sentences in your CSO meeting and throughout the day. Use positive and affirming words, thoughts, and emotions that describe what you want instead of what you don't.

It may take you some time to recognize counterproductive patterns of speaking. Many of us do this unconsciously, and it takes some effort to change it. It's oftentimes helpful to ask someone who supports your success if they'll read your CSO letters and provide suggestions for improving the language. As you become more consistent in using positive words it will become easier for you to notice anything that isn't supporting what you want.

If you experience challenges as you use this practice, don't get discouraged. Change takes time. As you persist with the practice, write down any questions you have and put them to one side. I can assure you that more understanding will follow as you use the practice daily. When you go back to those questions later, many times you will notice that the answers have revealed themselves as you've stayed the course. Miraculous demonstrations are on the verge of breaking through for you, and your focus on the right words will help them manifest sooner. Your CSO practice is the key to receiving all that you desire.

Exercise

Think of a challenge in your business or personal life that you'd like to change. Write a short, one-sentence statement about it. For example,

> I don't want to lose any more sales to my competitors.

In looking at the sentence you've written, ask yourself what the outcome would be if that problem didn't exist. Write down two or three affirmative statements that support what you want to experience. Affirm that good is available to you, your business, and everyone concerned. For example,

Thank you, CSO, that my company now meets our sales goals of $_____ easily and effortlessly. I am so grateful that our employees, customers, suppliers, and vendors all work together flawlessly to complete what's required for a fair exchange of value. Thank you that our company thrives and prospers as we grow to serve a larger number of customers, who thrive and prosper as well.

Use the process described above to analyze each of the statements in your most recent CSO gratitude letter. Are they speaking words of gratitude for something positive that you want? Do they mention anything you don't want, such as a problem employee not harming your business? If so, change them by thinking about what you would experience if that problem were removed. Write your revised gratitude statements in your next CSO letter.

Using Denials
to Support Your Good

Denial is a putting away of the mental error and an entering into conscious relaxation of both mind and body.

—Charles Fillmore, *Christian Healing*

As we've seen, using affirmations supports you in preparing to receive the good you want. This is not a new theory, but one based on business, social, and religious practices that have developed over centuries. Edna Miriam Lister, an early twentieth-century writer and religious leader, believed that psychology and metaphysics shared a common idea in the subject of affirmations and denials. Both schools of thought used a similar approach to healing and changing situations. If people wanted to effect change, be healed of a disease, or attract something different, they must "deny" the condition or disease and follow it with a statement of what they want, called an "affirmation."

Dr. Joseph Dispenza, author of numerous books on the power of thought, explains it this way: "Our thoughts have a direct connection to our direct level of health. Thoughts make a chemical. If you have happy thoughts, then you're producing chemicals that make you feel happy. It you have negative thoughts, angry thoughts, or insecure thoughts, those thoughts make chemicals to make you feel how you're thinking."

This is exciting news. We have the power to change our circumstances, our health, and how we feel simply by using our words, thoughts, and emotions. Affirmations and denials are tools to support the change process.

Using affirmations alone can bring you a long way on your journey toward your good. But adding denials, or a strong claim that anything that is not for your good is removed, is a powerful way to help eliminate negative beliefs, fears, or any other thoughts that arise and appear to be blocking your path.

To illustrate this, let's say that a businessman would like to increase sales this year in his company to $2 million. He may affirm: "I am grateful that my business now produces increased sales of a minimum of $2 million dollars this year easily, joyfully, and successfully. All of those related to my business benefit by it."

The businessman repeats this affirmation of the "what" that he wants as his good and imagines having it. The next step of the process is up to the CSO to provide the "how" to get to the good that the businessman desires. The CSO creates the path. As you'd expect, the businessman may feel a nudge or flash to take the next step—make a telephone call, go to different trade shows, learn something new, or talk to certain customers for more business or referrals. He'll do whatever the CSO leads him to do with confidence, knowing that he is on the path toward the good that he desires.

Now, let's assume that the businessman has been reading reports about the slow economy and also hearing stories about the increased success that his competitors are having. Meanwhile, his business has not achieved the sales goals they planned for last year. The man has a choice: focus on these situations as a reason for failure, or focus on his good as the success that he wants.

To gain success, the man must demolish any doubts and fears that he has before he states what he wants. Those statements could include, "I deny any lack of sales in my business. There is no limit to the amount of prosperity and abundance that is available in this universe. Therefore, there is no limit to the success and increased sales for my business. I am grateful that the CSO leads me to do that which I'm supposed to do, and sales for my business increase substantially to a minimum of $2 million this year. All who are related to my business benefit by it."

Hooray! The man has crushed the ideas that the economy and competitors have any influence on his success. His good is assured as the CSO creates the right path to the good that the man desires, and the man follows the directions.

It's very important that you always follow a denial with an affirmation. Otherwise, you'll be using your words only in relation to the problem. When we do that, we attract and receive more of what we're focusing on, more of the problem. Remember the story about my problem employee in the prior chapter? I prayed the problem and, as a result, got more of what I didn't want. Be specific and direct in composing your denials and affirmations so the subconscious has clear direction.

Other examples of denials followed by affirmations are "I deny any appearance of lack and loss. I am grateful that our products are being sold easily and successfully to the right buyers, giving perfect satisfaction," or "I deny any appearance of my making a mistake in this situation. The CSO as universal power transforms every decision of my past and present into my good today without delay."

Denials followed by affirmations assist you in changing situations that may be fearful or overwhelming. Remember, while we can't always control our thoughts, we can control our words. Repeat your well-worded denials and affirmations out loud. Use denials and affirmations when your thoughts overwhelm you with fears and doubts. Drown out the worried mind with your words, even if you don't believe them right away. Persist.

According to psychologist, author, and success coach Linda Sapadin, PhD, "Setting a goal and making a plan (i.e., what to do, when to do it, how to do it) can be a big help. Sure, you can just make a list, but saying it out loud focuses your attention, reinforces the message, controls your runaway emotions, and screens out distractions. Top athletes do this all the time by telling themselves, 'Keep your head down. Keep your eye on the ball. Breathe.' It works well for them, why not for you?"

As we discussed earlier, it is difficult to state one thing out loud and think a contrary thing at the same time. The spoken word will always win out. If a fearful thought pops up, deny its appearance and state your affirmations out loud.

You may have to repeat denials and affirmations dozens of times the first day, and you may not believe what you're saying. In the following days, you'll find that you need to do it fewer times because the fearful thoughts have slowed down and shown up less often. One day in the future, you will very confidently believe your denials and affirmations, and the negative and fearful thoughts will rarely show themselves. Eventually, there will be nothing to deny and you will have peace as you become that much closer to the good that you want.

Exercise

Write down a denial regarding an obstacle that may appear to be preventing or slowing your good from manifesting now. For example, "I deny any lack in my business success due to increased competition."

Write down an affirmation describing the good that you want to have. For example, "My divine partnership with the CSO ensures my business success, and I easily and joyfully receive increased revenues of a minimum of 25 percent or $350,000 this year."

Now add the two together, with the denial coming before the affirmation:

> I deny any lack in my business success due to increased competition. My divine partnership with the CSO ensures my business success, and I easily and joyfully receive increased revenues of a minimum of 25 percent or $350,000 this year.

Write your denial and affirmation on a card and put it somewhere that you can easily access. Read what you've written out loud whenever a fearful thought or obstacle comes to mind.

Facing Fears Fearlessly

If you are pained by external things, it is not they that disturb you, but your own judgment of them. And it is in your power to wipe out that judgment now.
— Marcus Aurelius, *Meditations*

It's wonderful that you've learned how to use denials and affirmations to remove situation-specific fears and doubts. These are powerful tools to have in your kit to obliterate obstacles and unblock channels. So what do you do when the CSO gives you a lead but you're not sure if you should take the directed step? You may be fearful of the unknown and can't help making judgments about it. This is the part of the practice that takes the most courage.

Often, you'll get a lead and won't be sure that it's really a lead. You don't know the final outcome. Your mind starts to wander to worst-case scenarios. You may freeze up in fear and do nothing. How should you handle this?

To begin, I first try "throwing a fleece" with the strong belief that the added information will get me the clarification that I want. Remember, "throwing a fleece" is asking the CSO for another sign to confirm a course of action that you're to take. I ask the CSO to give me a sign in a very obvious way. You can ask for as many leads as you need, but once your hunch is sufficiently confirmed, you must act on it. Don't hide behind fleeces to avoid making a move you know might be tough.

I get confirmation of leads in many different ways. I have driven by a billboard with a message that seemed to be for me. I've seen a headline in a newspaper that answered my question, or a friend has called to give me the message that I was seeking. I'll be directed to learn something new at a workshop or to drive across town. The key here is that I'm expecting and watching for the CSO to let me know what to do in response to my request. Oftentimes, other people or methods will deliver the messages to me. I notice those messages because there is a confirming feeling within me when I see or hear them.

Now let's look at some other tools you can use to overcome the fear that sometimes arises when it's time to take action on a lead from the CSO.

Avoid Future Tripping

Imagine that you've gotten another clear lead from the CSO, but you still don't know the outcome of taking the step. What will you do? Some of us stop and think about all the possible outcomes that taking that step could have, and in doing so, we may realize that many of the possibilities are not what we'd like to have. We're making a fearful judgment about the future, which I call "future tripping." But since we've already learned that whatever we put our attention on will manifest in our lives, you want to move away from this fear by either asking the CSO for another lead or taking an action faith step. The point here is to either do one or the other; don't sit in a place of indecisive fear. Ask for a lead or take the action.

For example, a friend of mine owns a lot of rental properties. One of her apartments had been unrented for longer than was normal, and she was worried by not having that income to offset the mortgage payments. She had already tapped into a significant amount of her savings to cover the costs and was imagining more than one unpleasant possible outcome of not getting the apartment rented.

I asked her if she had felt any leads or hunches to do something recently. She said that she did have a strong feeling to purchase a new overhead light for the dining room. At first she dismissed the idea—there were too many empty apartments on the market and not enough renters in the area. What difference would an overhead light make with that kind of competition? She was also fearful about spending any more money on the unit since she was losing money on it already.

I told my friend that I knew the CSO could direct the right renter her way. She needed to deny the appearance of too much rental inventory and thank the CSO for the perfect renter now. She needed to ask for another lead, to "throw a fleece," to see what the CSO had to say about buying the light. Later that day, she started to thank the CSO out loud with affirmative statements for the perfect renter showing up to rent her unit. She denied the many other apartment units blocking the perfect renter from wanting to rent her unit. And she asked the CSO if she was to buy the light or if there was anything else she should do to enable the unit to be rented. She kept this practice up and made the statements out loud dozens of times per day, whenever a fearful thought came up.

Two days later, she got a $25-off coupon from a local home store in the mail with a picture of a beautiful dining room light on the mailer. She said that she could feel that the pictured light needed to be hung in her unit and could imagine the warmth of the room with the new light. She reconfirmed her fear about spending any more money on her unit since she was already having difficulty paying the mortgage. I told her that I thought the coupon was an answer to her request for another lead and that it was time to show action faith and courage. She needed to face her fear and demonstrate her belief that the perfect renter would show up.

She drove to the home store, repeating her denials and affirmations, and bought the light. Within a week of installing it, the perfect renter called her after seeing her for rent sign in front of the building. The renter agreed to pay $50, or 7 percent more per month, if he could use the staged dining and living room furniture that she had in the unit. She was delighted, since she didn't want to have to move the furniture that had been left by the previous renter. The new renter also signed a two-year lease.

My friend showed courage and faced her fear after she got the lead to purchase the light. If you get a lead and are still fearful, go ahead and ask for another lead to confirm the direction that you're receiving from the CSO rather than doing nothing.

As you become more comfortable with this daily practice, you'll find that many of the fears that you thought you'd have to face will disappear. For example, Fred was a customer of mine who was very upset about a situation involving what he perceived as poor performance by our products and poor customer service from our employees. Our employees told me that Fred had yelled at them for a problem that our products didn't cause but did affect the performance of our products. He had been unkind to everyone who had talked to him.

In my daily practice, I asked the CSO for a lead. It was clear when Fred's face came to mind that I needed to meet with him. I wasn't looking forward to the meeting. I was afraid that Fred would be as upset with me as he had been with our employees. Knowing that I had to face the fear, I began using my words dozens of times before seeing Fred: "Dear true self of Fred, I bless you, I love you, I forgive you, and I release you. I know that you are receiving your highest and best good at all times and that all of the systems provided by our company are working well for you. I am so grateful we are working harmoniously together and have a great professional relationship. All who are related to this relationship benefit by it."

When I walked in to meet with Fred, he was perfectly delightful. He was especially grateful that I, as the CEO of our company, traveled to see him. We went over all of the problems in a calm and productive way. He mentioned that the problem he thought we had caused had been resolved and he was sorry for blaming our team. Prior to leaving, Fred gave me a purchase order for more software to be installed at a new location. He said how grateful he was to be working with a team that cared so much about him and his company. We would be welcome to bring any potential customers to his site to see our products in action. He would give us a great reference.

Approaching this fear prepared with the right words and actions made it so there was nothing fearful to face. This practice of preparedness and intention can work in all kinds of situations. Acknowledge your fears when they arise, but don't allow the unknown future to cripple what can always be a better outcome with the help of your CSO.

Dig Ditches to Receive Leads

Sometimes, with less clear direction and only a hunch, I do what I call "digging a ditch," which means that I start moving in what I think is the direction while continuing to ask for more leads along the way. "Digging ditches" is based on a Bible story in 2 Kings 3. The prophet Elisha has great respect for King Jehoshaphat of Judah, who comes to him with other kings when they and their troops have run out of water. Elisha conveys God's instructions to the kings to dig ditches in the desert. The king was shocked to hear these instructions, but Elisha assured him that this was the direction from God. The kings and their troops dug the ditches even though they couldn't see how they'd receive water. In doing so, they showed action faith that God would fill the ditches with water somehow. The story goes on to say that the ditches were filled with water even though it had not rained. Could they have hit a spring or underground river? That's possible, but they still would have needed direction on where to dig. The faith to follow God's directions through Elisha's message and dig the right number of ditches in the right places resulted in enough water for the troops. The water was the good that they desired. The "how" that made it appear was left up to God.

I dig my ditches, too. I do something, buy something, or take some action as I feel directed to do by the CSO even when I don't see how it will get me closer to the good that I desire. This shows my action faith.

For example, I once faced a decision on adding a new product to our catalog, and I didn't know whether or not my company was supposed to become a distributor for this particular product. I asked the CSO for a lead and didn't feel any immediate hunch about what to do. I simply didn't feel guided one way or the other. I continued to ask daily for an unmistakable sign. A few days later, I saw an advertisement for a one-day sale on airfare from my city to the location of the manufacturer's United States office. The cost of the plane ticket was 75 percent less than the normal price. I felt a strong hunch to "dig a ditch" and buy the ticket. I scheduled a meeting for the next week with the manufacturer. I also asked my business partner to go with me.

In preparation for the meeting, I proclaimed a desire to the CSO for more leads: "CSO, if our company is to become the distributor for this product, show up in an obvious way and make the deal easy and joyful to complete. And if we're not to become the distributor, slam the door on this deal and I will know that something better will show up for our company's highest and best good."

While in the meeting with the manufacturer, I felt a strong urge to outline a deal structure that was unfamiliar to me but seemed to be a good plan for both our companies. It unfolded methodically in my mind with such clarity that I knew it was the right plan. The manufacturer hadn't heard of a plan like the one I'd outlined, but he liked it. He agreed to my terms.

Later, my business partner asked where I'd gotten the idea to present this new deal, since it was so unusual. I replied that it must have been the CSO, since I had never even heard of a deal like it. I described what I experienced in the meeting and how a feeling of confidence enveloped me as the words tumbled out of my mouth. We both agreed that it was a great deal. I'm happy to report that this plan worked out for our mutual good over several years, and I have my CSO to thank for it.

If new leads or hunches show up as an intuitive nudge to buy something, learn something new, or make a phone call to a client/employee/vendor, do it and continue in the direction that you feel led. All the while you're taking those steps, make statements out loud to the CSO:

- » "I'm going to go this way, CSO. Correct me if there's a better way."

- » "CSO, I feel that you've guided me to take this step. Thank you for showing up to confirm that I'm on the right path, or slam the door and point me in a better direction toward the good that I want."

- » "Your way, not my way. I know that I am divinely led with each and every step I take. Thank you for giving me a definite lead toward my good."

This practice is "digging your ditch" to be filled with your good.

As you continue facing your fears and taking action in faith as led by your CSO, you will find that it becomes easier to do. Your confidence and trust in the CSO will become stronger, and you'll feel assured as you take each step toward the good that you desire.

Cast the Burden on the CSO

Another technique that you can use to face your fears is to cast the burden on the CSO. Casting the burden is a way to impress the subconscious and release you from the burden of fear. As we work in partnership with the CSO, we commit to asking for help when we need it or when we're in the middle of a situation and can't see a way out.

Remember, your job is to establish the "what" that you want and to follow the steps of the daily practice. The job of the CSO is to develop the path and guide you to take steps to manifest your desires. If there is a burden that blocks your way, you should give it up and ask that the CSO handle it. That responsibility is in the job description of the CSO. Let the CSO do its job and make the path clear.

When a fearful or negative situation is presented, say, "I cast this burden of [resentment, lack, jealousy, anger] on the CSO within, and I go free to be [successful, loving, happy, harmonious, financially free, at peace, forgiving] easily and joyfully, with grace and in perfect ways."

Make the statement over and over until the thought or idea of the situation gives you peace. You will know that you have peace when the situation or person has "safe passage" through your mind. Safe passage means that you have no emotional reaction when thinking of the situation or person. It could take dozens or hundreds of repetitions until you are at peace, but stick with it!

Include "With Grace and in Perfect Ways"

Sometimes our fears can limit us from imagining all the possible pathways to our good. By adding the phrase "with grace in perfect ways," you're allowing the CSO to create a situation that can deliver good for you and all concerned—and sometimes it's even a better outcome than you originally considered. By adding "with grace in perfect ways" to your affirmations, you open the door to the CSO's possible outcomes.

For example, a friend of mine wanted to live in a beautiful home on Capitol Hill in Seattle. She dreamed of living in a gorgeous mansion and would often drive by the homes proclaiming, "I am so grateful that God is orchestrating my life so that I live in a gorgeous mansion here on Capitol Hill. I have lots of room and a wonderful kitchen to prepare delicious meals for my friends. We all have a great time together."

She would spend time thinking about the dinners she would serve to her friends and the fun that she would have preparing them and entertaining. She was filled with great joy when thoughts of welcoming family and friends to her home would come to mind.

Within a month of beginning her affirmations, my friend found herself in a troubling financial position that required her to find a new place to live. She was given a house-sitting job in a big mansion on Capitol Hill. She enjoyed living there and having her friends over while the owners were out of town. However, she realized later that she wanted to own her own home. She also recognized that her fears about money may have contributed to her getting into financial distress.

She began to be more specific in her desires and added, "with grace and in perfect ways" to her affirmations. She decided that she wanted to live in a home she owned, be in a loving community that was supportive, and have financial freedom with more than enough money and resources to support her. She began to change her words to voice what she really wanted: "I am so grateful that God is my supply and affords me to live in and own a gorgeous home that is perfect for me and my family. I have lots of room and a wonderful kitchen to prepare delicious meals for joyful celebrations. I have all of the resources to easily support my lifestyle filled with love, ease, and joy. All of this manifests with grace and in perfect ways."

As a result of this affirmative prayer, my friend received an invitation to take a new job in Oregon and live near her parents. She showed courage and acted on the invitation.

Now, a few years later, she can say she received her good. She purchased a fabulous home with her family, and her parents live nearby. She lives in a community that loves and supports her, and she works at a well-paying job that makes it easy to fund her lifestyle. When she let go of specifics about the house and location and did the work to eliminate fears about money, she prepared to let her CSO provide for her good "with grace and in perfect ways." She received an even greater experience of the things that were most important to her.

The CSO gets involved in the situation when you've made room for it to be there. If you've limited the CSO or you are filled with fear or negative emotions, you can't see all the ways in which you can experience your good. I had a teacher put it this way: If you have a turbulent body of water, you could throw the Space Needle in the water and not see a rippling effect. If you have a calm body of water, the smallest stone hitting the surface will be easy to spot. It's the same with turbulent emotions. When you trust that the CSO is working for your good and you cast the burden and go free, you're making your thinking and emotions like a calm body of water. The CSO then can throw in a pebble as an intuitive lead, and you'll receive it. You will notice the lead because you're calm enough to do so.

Several years ago I felt a strong lead to build a software company with a previous partner based on customer requirements that no available software could provide. We both had no idea where we would find the skilled software developers we needed. We hired another person from our industry who had some contacts that we hoped would lead us in the right direction. I had doubts and fears about our ability to attract the right people and imagined the worst-case scenario: "Since we're based in Seattle, Microsoft's backyard, we won't be able to afford quality developers." My mind was filled with negative thoughts that left no room to allow the CSO in to help.

After a few days going from fear to faith and back again, I remembered to rely on the CSO as my partner. I knew the CSO had already provided conditions for our business to do well. I had to cast my burden of fear and doubt on the CSO and create an environment for the CSO to work successfully. I used my words to support this partnership and thanked the CSO for guiding me and the right developers to work together at our company. I denied the appearance that I wasn't smart enough or experienced enough to hire the right developers. I cast the burden on the CSO of finding the right employees and affirmed that they were on their way to us with grace and in perfect ways.

The right employees did show up without my having to place any advertisements. They contacted us through others we knew in the industry who had heard we were looking for help. They were a perfect fit for our business, yet they lived in San Antonio, Texas. We let go of the requirement to have everyone be in Seattle and made the decision to open an office in San Antonio. We received tremendous tax and expense savings as a result. We got an even greater experience of good by letting the CSO do its job.

It is not in your job description to handle any burdens whatsoever. Turn all burdens over to the CSO and go forth, free to be successful, loving, harmonious, happy, radiant, and detached from the tyranny of fear. Identify your good, ask for leads, follow directions, and receive your good. That's your only job in the relationship.

I encourage you to start asking the CSO for leads and direction now, if you haven't already done so. Use the techniques above to eliminate fears or burdens, and go free to realize a higher and greater good. If you feel a lead to do something, do it. You can throw fleeces and dig ditches to get confirming leads, hunches, and intuitive direction from the CSO along the way. You will be directed to do what's necessary, and your good will show up.

Exercise

Think of a situation in the past that seemed scary or too big for you to handle. What did you do when you had to face it? Knowing what you know now about facing fearful situations, how would you handle that situation differently? What would be your desired outcome? Create an affirmation to neutralize the situation described above, and state how you would "walk up to it fearlessly." Create a "cast the burden" statement to gain more freedom.

Other Ways to Unlock Your Good

Our deepest fear is not that we are inadequate. Our deepest fear is that we are powerful beyond measure. It is our light, not our darkness that most frightens us.
—Marianne Williamson, *A Return to Love*

What do you do when you're using all the spiritual steps, practicing every day, eliminating fear and doubt, and still nothing is happening? Chances are, there's a deep-rooted belief that you're not consciously aware of that is blocking your good from arriving now. There may be an unconscious self-imposed boundary or limit on what you feel comfortable receiving. This unconscious belief usually sounds something like "I am not worthy" or "I don't deserve this." If you have a hidden limit and you're asking the CSO to help you receive something greater than what you believe to be possible, you may experience a delay in receiving your good or you may not be able to hold on to the good once you finally get it. Following are a couple examples of what this looks like.

In 2006, a Welsh-born man was flat broke and used one of his last dollars to buy a lottery ticket. He won £1.3 million ($1.9 million) and spent all his winnings on a trip to the Canary Islands, his wedding, and a new home. A year and a half later, he was working at McDonald's flipping burgers. Could a mental equivalent issue have caused this outcome? Perhaps he wasn't yet ready to accept all the good that was presenting itself to him, and thus he subconsciously rejected it and was unable to hold on to his winnings.

In another example, a single mother on welfare cashed a check from a Canadian Lottery and Gaming Corp. for CAD$10,569,000. She subsequently spent her winnings on a big house, fancy cars, designer clothes, lavish parties, exotic trips, handouts to family, and loans to friends. In less than a decade, she was back to riding the bus, working part-time, and living in a rented house. Could an unconscious belief that she was not worthy of that good fortune have been the cause of her actions as well? I believe that's a possibility.

It's vitally important that you prepare yourself to be comfortable with the good that you want and welcome it, as unconscious limits can keep you from receiving it. Here are some steps you can take to make the things you want more familiar to you and to remove any unconscious limitations you may have.

Experience What You Want

If a new home and car are some of the things that you have identified as the good that you want, go to open houses and experience the homes of your dreams. Walk around them and imagine what it would be like to live there, to drive into the driveway, walk through the front door, and stock the refrigerator after shopping. Sit on the couch and feel yourself in that space. Go to a car dealership and test-drive the car you felt you could never afford before. Notice how you feel driving this car. Know that it could be yours and that it's okay because the CSO knows the path to help you receive it.

If you want more satisfaction and fulfillment at work, go to a class, seminar, or workshop that includes people who you feel portray the person you'd like to be. For example if you'd like to be a PhD with published work, read success stories or go to seminars with PhDs with published works. See what they're like. Become familiar with their environment. Listen to their conversations and to speakers who are sharing information with them. Imagine that you're operating in that same environment comfortably and confidently.

If you're interested in being an artist who makes a good living doing what you love, read about the career paths of successful artists and go to the places they hang out. See them, meet them, and find out about the journey that got them where they are now. Prepare for your good. See yourself doing what you want and receiving that good, too.

These are just a few examples, but the point is that once you have identified your good, make yourself ready and comfortable to receive it by experiencing as much of it as possible today. In this way, you are signaling to your unconscious mind that you are deserving of this good and that you know how to receive it.

Worthiness Mantra

To support your excursions that show tangible samples of the things that you want, affirm your worthiness to receive this good:

> Thank you, CSO, that I am a perfect and worthy creation that is unique and very good. What the CSO had done for others' success and prosperity it now does for me and more.

Repeat this with conviction whenever an old thought of unworthiness or limitation comes up. You'll know this has happened if your thoughts say: "It's too good to be true. I can never have/be/experience that." You can consciously drown out this negative thought with your words.

Increase Your Visualization

Sometimes you can't actually go and experience manifestations of the good that you want. In these rare instances, there is still something you can do to undo any unconscious limiting beliefs you may be holding. Remember the exercise on imaging as part of the daily practice? Use imaging to make yourself familiar and comfortable with the items you want. This will help you to vibrate at the level of those things and welcome them into your life. Once an item is welcome, what you proclaim will eventually produce stronger feelings and new beliefs. You'll become magnetic to receiving it, and your new beliefs will welcome it to stay.

Don't Force Anything

Let me be clear on something: I am not advocating that you do something to force the good to manifest. In other words, don't go out and purchase something big and go into debt, thinking that the CSO will make everything right for you. Don't quit your job and hope that the CSO will find you a new one. Attempting to force an outcome in this way is not a part of the seven-step path. Remember, your job is to prepare for and welcome the good that you want, and then wait for the CSO to guide you down the path to get there.

You establish the "what" that you want to have and experience. The CSO takes care of the "how" to create the path for it to happen and gives you directions on the next steps to take. You will be much better able to recognize leads and do what the CSO leads you to do after you've removed any unconscious blocks you have. The additional tips I have shared here—experience what you want, the worthiness mantra, and increase your visualization—will prepare you to receive a new and higher level of good into your life.

Other Examples of Unconscious Limits

I have a wonderful friend whom some would call very wealthy. He clearly doesn't have any hidden limits or unworthiness issues about money and is quite generous. He has told me often that he'd like to find the right life partner. But when proclaiming that expression of good for himself, he would follow quickly with statements like, "No one would want to spend their life with an old guy like me," or "I've been living alone for so long, I wouldn't be able to change my habits to have a successful relationship." I know that part of this belief stemmed from his perceived failures in prior relationships, but there may have been other limiting factors contributing to that feeling, too.

We discussed the use of his words to create the life that he wants, but to no avail. He says that he can't change the way he thinks. Unfortunately, my friend is stuck in this attitude and is still single today. I continue to hope that my friend recognizes that the good he desires can be his if he shifts his thinking to enable it to happen.

Perhaps you know someone who feels that a situation is beyond repair or they're too old or stuck in their ways to change their attitude. As you use the CSO practice and incorporate the principles outlined in this book, you'll be able to share with them examples of your success at changing your old habits and beliefs. You may become the ray of hope that they need. None of us are here to change others. That's not our job. We're only here to change ourselves. The best that we can offer to is to support others the best we can. We can also believe that there is a good for them and they ought to have it.

Several years ago, I realized that I had been holding a belief that one had to work hard and sacrifice spending time with family and friends in order to be successful. As a result of this hidden belief I declined invitations to events, using phrases like, "I'm too busy to attend," or "I've got too much work to do." I wanted great relationships, but that wasn't possible as long as I was holding a deep-rooted belief that I couldn't be successful and have ample free time simultaneously. But once I had uncovered this belief, I knew I needed to eliminate it and create a new good for my life.

I took a class about mastering the self and made time to talk with other successful businesspeople to learn how they managed their work and family lives. I discovered many successful people had lives that were in much greater balance than mine. One man, who had raised over $250 million with a new public company, said that he made sure to make dinner for his family every day he was in town. That amazed me. I began to believe if he can do it, I can too.

I used my daily practice to proclaim a new good for me. I began to deny the appearance that work got in the way of spending time celebrating with family and friends. I created affirmative statements about my gratitude for work: that it was easy, fun, successful, prosperous, and satisfying, and that all of my professional and personal relationships were harmonious and in balance. I repeated the affirmative statements out loud when old negative habits and beliefs would pop up. I surrounded myself with successful people who were living balanced and healthy lives. This helped me to become more familiar with and welcome that same kind of good into my life.

After several weeks of using this practice with consistency, my businesses' success continued and my relationships improved. I was easily able to get the help and support I needed from others, get my work done in less time, enjoy my work more, and feel increased happiness. My family was happy to see me home earlier, and I went on fun weekend outings with them without taking calls from work.

Another example of a belief that can be hidden has to do with leaving things unfinished, or what I call a "belief in incompletion." If your habit is to start things but not complete them, you may be unconsciously expecting the same to happen when you start on any new goal for the good that you want.

For example, I knew a woman who was experiencing delay in receiving the good she had been asking for in her business. Although she had been experiencing a few small demonstrations, there wasn't a feeling of peace or consistency in their arrival. They fell short of her expectations and felt incomplete.

She then acknowledged that while she had some great business practices in other areas of her work, she had a pattern of starting new projects and leaving them unfinished. I thought this could be part of the reason why she hadn't yet received her good; as she would start projects and not finish them, she was directing the universal power to do the same.

She was excited about this revelation. At her office, she set to work to finish an employee manual she had begun months before. She declared affirmative statements of truth about ease and joy in the completion of her manual. She blocked off time in her calendar to do the work and finished the manual over the next few weeks and afterward felt happy and proud of the work she had done.

Within three days of distributing the completed manual to her employees, her company received a large new order from a customer that her sales team had briefly met at a trade show. Her company hadn't done any follow-up meetings with the customer. Regardless, the customer told the sales team he felt confident their company could do the job based on another happy customer's experience. This was a great demonstration of success. Would that order have come in anyway? Maybe. But the fact that it came in when it did was confirmation for my friend that she shouldn't leave things unfinished.

There can be a number of hidden beliefs that don't support you in receiving the good you want. Take the time to search for any patterns in your past that may be limiting you. The first step to gaining freedom is recognizing the hidden belief. See if you can identify a pattern or behavior that is repeating itself and not serving your highest good. When you change that behavior, you are sending a signal to the universal power to do the same.

Conflicts as a Block to Receiving Your Good

We've already discussed the importance of forgiveness. Similarly, having ongoing conflicts with others can generate fear and block your good from manifesting. When experiencing conflict with another person, one way to release this is to write to his or her divine "true self," the part that is influenced by the all-knowing universal power.

To do this, you will need to use a write-and-speak technique similar to what you learned for the CSO daily practice, but direct your attention to the divine true self of the person you'd like to influence. Use the following as an outline:

Dear divine true self of _____,

I bless you, I love you, and I give great thanks that you are now _____ for all of our good. Everyone who is related to this now benefits from it.

I mentioned earlier that I started a new business a little more than a year after I sold my interest in a previous company. Three years after I had completed my noncompete period, my old company brought a lawsuit against my new company and me and issued a press release about it.

I knew that we had not done anything wrong and engaged an attorney to help us. Because my confidence in the CSO partnership was strong, I didn't go immediately to a place of panic like I would have in the past. I went directly to the CSO and asked for guidance.

To start, I gathered information from my attorney about the case. He assured me that since an injunction hadn't been obtained by my former company we could continue to operate our business. In my daily practice, I felt guided by the CSO to consider what the motivation of my former company could be. Maybe they felt threatened because our company had been winning in most of the competitive situations against their company. We were also converting their existing customers to purchase new products and services from our company. All of this was being done fairly, as the customers were looking for better products and services. Perhaps the other company thought a lawsuit would slow our growth and success.

Every motivation I thought of was a fear-based action. Because of this, I started to increase my affirmative truth statements to support my belief that there was enough business for both companies. I continued to work with the CSO to dissolve the lawsuit and create an environment where both companies could thrive.

My attorney did his job and handled the legal aspects expertly. I did what I felt was my job. I partnered with the CSO and wrote and spoke the following out loud daily: "Dear true self of all related to my former company, I bless you, I love you, I forgive you, and I give great thanks that you are now dissolving this lawsuit between us quickly, easily, and completely. All related to this within both our companies are now freed and benefit from it. All legal fees spent by my company are now restored to us with grace and in perfect ways."

Over the five months that I worked with the CSO for the dissolving of the lawsuit and forgave everyone related to my former company, our sales grew 35 percent. More and more customers signed contracts with us, and our installations were smooth and on time. I don't know the exact motivations of the customers, but it's my belief that as I gave out energy with thoughts of forgiveness and prosperity, I received prosperity in return. When the lawsuit ended, our legal fees were more than restored.

If you have identified a conflict as preventing you from receiving your good, try writing a letter to that person's divine true self. Even though you will never send this letter, it creates an atmosphere of peace and balance, opening you up to the good the CSO has in store for you.

In addition to writing the letter, you can also ask the CSO to give you a lead on what to do specifically to remedy the issue: "Thank you, CSO, for revealing to me anything I should do in this situation. Give me a definite lead. Show me what to do." I did exactly that in this next example.

My company was a successful distributor for a manufacturer supplier. For whatever reason, the supplier decided they didn't want a different distributor to sell their products at the end of their contract. Without warning, the canceled distributor served my company and me with a lawsuit. To say that I was surprised was an understatement. I did not go to a place of love and forgiveness right away. I went into fear and panic mode. This was a huge company suing my small business for something that we weren't even a part of.

My mind raced. "How could this happen to me? This is so unfair! They are a huge company, and this is going to place a financial strain on us that could put us out of business. They are such bullies." Fear was driving me to give up my power to the large company. I did not have any kind thoughts for the large company or their representatives.

Within a couple hours of my fearful pity party, I retreated to a quiet place and calmed down. I had a meeting with the CSO to ask for guidance on how I should respond. The first lead was to contact my attorney, who would gather the legal information in a calm manner. The second lead was to put myself in the shoes of the company that brought the lawsuit against us. Perhaps they wanted to put pressure on their supplier to reconsider. They most likely realized that my company wouldn't sell the supplier's products until the lawsuit was over. I never learned what their actual motivation was, but these were possibilities that I considered.

I recognized that fear could be the underlying motivator. The distributor didn't want to lose their supplier. They needed to be able to serve their customers. How could they do that without a supplier?

As I considered that possibility, my heart shifted. I knew that there could be some good for us all because good from the CSO is infinite. I asked the CSO for a lead. What I received was the idea to practice forgiveness for the other distributor and outline a possible resolution for the supplier.

I started with the forgiveness statement, "Dear divine true self of all that are related to your company, I bless you, I love you, I forgive you, I release you. I give great thanks that you are dissolving this lawsuit between us. I know that there is more than enough business in our industry for both our companies to thrive and prosper and that the right products and suppliers are available to us all. There is nothing to fear. All those related to this benefit from it."

Then I recommended a solution inspired by the CSO for our equipment supplier to consider. An agreement was reached, and it all worked out for everyone's good. My company was also reimbursed for all our legal fees.

It may be difficult to communicate calmly and lovingly with the CSO during difficult times such as these, but be persistent in your requests for leads and follow the directions you receive. You may get a lead to create a solution, like I did for the supplier and the other distributor.

When you work on resolving conflicts, there are a few points to keep in mind. Resolving conflict doesn't mean you give in to the other person's demands. You want to open your heart and come from a place of love rather than fear, but this doesn't mean you become a doormat. You are not able to control the other party's actions or reactions; the point here is to bring your intentions into alignment with the highest good for everyone involved.

In summary, becoming free from anything blocking your good is your objective. As you move out old beliefs, habits, and behaviors that are not serving you, more room becomes available for you to receive all that your heart desires. There is good for you waiting to pour into your life, and you deserve to have it. Unblock the channels to receive your good now.

Exercise

Examine your life up to this point and identify anything that has happened more than once that you'd like to change: relationships not working out long term, changes in your job that affect you adversely, health and diet goals that start out well but never reach fruition, company sales goals not being met no matter where you work. What steps could you employ to uncover any hidden beliefs that exist and establish a new belief to receive your good?

Describe a person in your business or personal life from whom you'd like to receive something or with whom you'd like to resolve an issue. (For example, complete a contract or lease, end a disagreement, or have a more harmonious and productive relationship.) Write a short affirmative statement and speak it out loud: "Dear divine true self of _____, I bless you, I love you, and I give great thanks that you are completing the contract between us in a mutually beneficial and harmonious way as soon as possible and that all benefit by it. There is an abundance of business available for both our companies to thrive and prosper."

Jump-Start Your Good
with Giving

It is one of the beautiful compensations of life that no man can sincerely help another without helping himself.

—Ralph Waldo Emerson

While you can't force your good to manifest instantly, there are actions you can take to help it arrive sooner. A great way to do this is to give out the same thing you want to receive. I know this may sound like a stretch, but keep an open mind.

Giving opens the way to receiving in any area of life. It could be money, love, peace, success, time—just about anything. To jump-start the flow of good into your life, start giving something that represents what you want to receive. Whatever you give out will come back to you in some form.

Deepak Chopra explains it this way: "The universe operates through dynamic exchange . . . giving and receiving are different aspects of the flow of energy in the universe. And in our willingness to give that which we seek, we keep the abundance of the universe circulating in our lives."

One of the first times I experienced this principlel was in college. As a student, I didn't have much money, but I wanted to have more. To jump-start my good, I decided to give more to others. Taking anything from the meager stipend I had was difficult back then, but I chose to buy a sandwich for a homeless person every day as I changed buses to go to work.

This giving made me feel like I was helping, and that made me feel good! Sometimes, I'd find money while walking on the street. Other times, someone would give me a gift because I helped him or her with a project. The net of these gifts was always in excess of the amount I spent on the sandwiches. This occurred every month without fail, and as a result I became sold on the principle of giving what we want to receive.

In my last business, I asked all employees to make a conscious commitment to working for the success of their coworkers, customers, suppliers and vendors, and our world. I assured them that in doing so, they would benefit in return. They all agreed to make that a conscious commitment, and they later reported that after doing so for one month, they all felt more satisfaction in their daily work—

not to mention additional sales. You see, our company received new business as a result of referrals from happy customers who said our employees were a joy to work with. In turn, our employees received bonuses as our profits increased. Our employees developed a new belief that desiring success for others would return the same to them. That made them happy, especially when they opened that bonus check.

I once had a student who manufactured and distributed health and beauty products to retail stores. She wanted to do well in business and decided to focus her energy on helping her customers do well in their business. During her store visits, she cleaned up and organized the shelves that contained her competitors' products, as well as her own. When her own employee asked why she was spending time straightening and organizing the competitions' products, my student explained that she wanted to do well in business and to do so she needed to help her customers do well in their business—and in this case, that included supporting her competitors' products. By accident, the store buyer overheard my student's explanation. The following week, my student was notified that the store buyer had arranged to give her additional business at four more of their stores in the area. My student's business grew by thousands of dollars in a delightful way!

And remember, you can use the principle of jump-starting your good with giving to receive the other good things you want to experience as well.

I have a friend who was feeling very unappreciated at work. She managed the accounting department in a large company, and morale and enthusiasm were low. She started practicing the simple seven-step process that she learned at one of my workshops and then decided to jump-start her good by appreciating others around her. She contacted family members and some of her employees to let them know how much she appreciated them. Within a week, her boss came down the hall and dropped to his knees and started waving his arms as a symbol of homage. He said out loud how grateful he was to my friend and her department for the great work they'd done in finding an accounting error that could have cost the company tens of thousands of dollars. Employees in her department saw this, and morale and enthusiasm improved even more. They all felt very appreciated.

According to Dr. Stephen Post, professor of preventive medicine and bioethics at Stony Brook University School of Medicine and the author of *The Hidden Gifts of Helping* and *Why Good Things Happen to Good People*, "Every great moral and spiritual tradition points to the truth that in the giving of self lies the discovery of a deeper self." Post goes on to say, "Creativity, meaning, resilience, health and even longevity can be enhanced as a surprising byproduct of contributing to the lives of others. This is perennial wisdom, and science now says it is so." Post focuses on the relationship between giving and happiness, longevity and health. To support your desire for success, happiness, longevity, and health, begin giving the same to others.

If you want more money, give more money. Give even a small amount to a place that you're spiritually, intellectually, or emotionally supported by. Any place or person that has had a positive impact on your growth and is valuable to you could be considered a place to give.

If you want more time, donate some of your time; be a greeter at an organization you belong to, volunteer at a place you appreciate, or help one of your children's teachers or coaches.

If you want more love, give out more love to others; call someone or email a note that tells them how much you appreciate them.

If you want better health, start giving better health to others; call a friend to take a walk, or cook a healthy meal for you and others to enjoy.

I understand that many people feel they can't give money because they struggle to pay all their expenses each month on the income they receive. Keep in mind that this attitude supports a fear-based belief in lack. I can assure you that if you make giving an intention and you partner with the CSO to show you how it can happen, you will be able to find an amount to give. Your giving will result in a greater increase for you.

Ask questions of yourself to discover the amount of money or time that you are comfortable giving with cheer and without fear. Whatever amount you decide to give will be perfect. I encourage you to make your giving consistent if you want to receive consistently in your life.

Just as important as giving more of what you want to receive is the act of being a good receiver. We're operating on the premise that what you give out you will get back from a different source. For giving to work, there has to be a receiver. Sometimes in order to unblock your good, you have to be the good receiver. What does it mean to be a good receiver? It means accepting the gift with gratitude.

If someone pays you a compliment, do you downplay it, ignore it, or decline it? If someone offers you a gift, do you decline or refuse it because you don't feel you deserve it or the person can't afford it? If you wanted to give someone a gift, wouldn't you want them to receive it with gratitude?

Keep in mind that by becoming a gracious receiver, you are completing the cycle of giving and receiving. All things in the universe are circulating, and your actions are part of that. As you give, you are preparing to receive. As you receive, you are allowing others to give and prepare to receive their good. Accept the gifts that are offered to you with gratitude. Look the giver in the eye and say thank you.

Exercise

Write down one sentence that describes something you want more of in your life and/or business. For example, "I want to implement one new creative idea that results in a new income stream for me."

How do you feel when you think of giving away money, time, love, friendship? What could you give today that rep resents what you'd like to have more of in your life?

To whom would you give it?

Conclusion

Congratulations! You now have all the tools necessary to partner effectively with the CSO and create a life filled with all the good you want. It's important to remember what your job is and what the CSO's job is in the partnership. Trust that each of you can do your job effectively.

You are to commit to having the CSO as your partner in business and life and determine the good that you want to receive. As part of your commitment to the partnership, agree to meet with the CSO and follow the agenda with the elements below for a minimum of thirty minutes each morning and throughout the day:

1. Read something uplifting.

2. Write gratitude statements for things that you have and want in a letter to the CSO.

3. Speak your truth as you read your letter out loud with emotion.

4. Imagine the experience of having the good that you desire.

5. Expect leads from the CSO to direct you to your good. Ask for additional leads.

6. Celebrate with a friend and record the events when your good shows up—nothing is too small.

7. End your day with gratitude and forgiveness. Forgive any situation, any person, and yourself for anything that needs to be forgiven in the past or present. Be grateful for all the good you have and will receive in your life.

Remember, the CSO's job is to create the path and circumstances leading you to the good you've identified and are grateful for, and to direct you down the path. Your job is to follow the leads.

The universal power has set up a marvelous life for each of us to enjoy and is always involved in our lives to the extent that we allow it. As you develop your daily practice and recognize that you will be directed toward the good you desire, you'll become less resistant and fearful in following the guidance from the CSO. Your level of peace, happiness, and prosperity will increase substantially.

Thank you for committing to make the CSO your partner in business and in life. You will find that you continue to grow and prosper with joy and fulfillment as you use the daily practice consistently. There is good for you, and you ought to have it. It's time for you to have it now.

May you be blessed and prosperous—it is your divine right!

Acknowledgments

I would like to express my sincere gratitude to my CSO and the many people who supported and encouraged me during the creation of this book

Thank you to my husband, Don Smith, who provided me with an incredible amount of love and support during the process of reading and commenting on more than a few drafts of my work in progress.

Thank you to my sister, Sharon Ramey, who created situations for me to begin teaching the success principles found in this book and who is my favorite person to celebrate with.

Thanks to the community at Center for Spiritual Living in Seattle and Dr. Kathianne Lewis for providing the environment that allows me to help more people to experience freedom and prosperity.

Thank you to Randy Davila of Hierophant Publishing, who saw something special in what I wanted to offer the world and gave me the ability to help a greater number of people achieve their goals for financial abundance and freedom. I would also like to thank Laura Matthews, Susie Pitzen, and Allison Jacob, all of whom helped me through the editing process.

Above all, I would like to thank my mother, Elizabeth McCarthy, who gave me my first metaphysical book thirty-two years ago and reminded me often that we live in an infinitely abundant universe that wants each of us to have the desires of our hearts. All we need to do is believe and receive them.

Blessings and love to you all.

Appendix

Life likes to be taken by the lapel and told, "I'm with you kid. Let's go!"

—Maya Angelou

I am delighted that you have made the commitment to partner with the all-knowing power in the universe. I know that you will experience more of the good things that you want in your life as you develop your relationship with your new partner. To help you get started right away with your daily practice, I've included a list of affirmations and suggested books.

Affirmations for Business and Life

As part of your daily CSO meeting, you will be creating affirmative statements for the writing and speaking sections. I use the statements below in my writing and throughout the day to support my daily practice. You're welcome to use these for inspiration as you create affirmations that are right for you. It's important that you use affirmations that create an emotional charge within you and that you are excited about.

To Experience Right Business Situations

» "The divine plan for my business unfolds perfectly."

» "Only what is true of the CSO is true of me. I am inspired and led to make right decisions quickly in every situation."

» "I am grateful that the CSO guides and directs me to experience my highest and best good at all times."

» "All who are related to my business benefit from it."

» "All that is for the highest and best good of me and my business manifests without delay, with grace and in perfect ways."

To Increase Success

» "The CSO now guides and directs me in all of my affairs, and my business is experiencing increased sales and profits."

» "The CSO goes before me, and my success is assured."

» "All our customers are happy, satisfied, and delighted with our products and services. They tell all their peers at other companies to buy from us, too. And they do."

» "My business takes off with a huge increase in sales. All related to this are blessed by it."

» "The CSO guides me to never-ending supply, and I accept and receive the huge success that is mine now."

To Obtain the Right Customers

» "Only those customers who are for our company's highest and best good now show up and purchase from us. All others find their good elsewhere."

- » "All our customers love us as we work toward our mutual success with excellence and kindness."

- » "Hundreds of new customers find their way to us and purchase our products easily and joyfully, with grace and in perfect ways."

- » "We are so blessed with increase and plenty as we bless with success our increasing number of customers."

- » "We are magnetic to our good and gratefully receive a 25 percent increase in new customers this quarter."

To Partner with the Right Suppliers

- » "Only those suppliers who are for our company's highest and best good provide us with service. All others find their good elsewhere."

- » "All suppliers work toward the good of our coworkers, our customers, and our world. They are benefited and happy as a result."

- » "Our suppliers are an expression of the CSO and treat us fairly as we work together in harmony and success."

- » "Our business attracts the right suppliers to help us thrive and prosper. All related to our businesses are blessed by it."

> » "What the CSO has intended for our good is now made manifest in our relationships with our right suppliers."

For Right Employees

> » "Only those employees who are for our company's highest and best good appear for us to hire. All others find their highest and best good elsewhere."

> » "All employees are happy and work in harmony and bless with success our coworkers, our customers, our suppliers and vendors, and our world in wonderful ways."

> » "Our employees use their creativity and talents in joyful ways to create, provide, implement, and support our flawless, superior, easy-to-use, and flawless products and services. All related to this are happy and blessed by it."

> » "All employees have perfect work and receive perfect pay."

> » "Only that which is true of the CSO is true of our employees. The CSO is all there is, and this is all good."

To Improve Relationships

> » "I cast all burdens of poor relationships on the CSO within. We all go free to be loving, harmonious, and detached from the tyranny of fear."

- » "Just as everything in universal power is harmonious and perfect, everything in my relationships is harmonious and perfect. All are happy."

- » "Everyone and every situation is a strong and valuable link in the chain of good for me and my business. I value and love everyone."

- » "Adverse people and situations are a part of my good. The CSO works through all people to bring my good to pass."

- » "I love everyone and everyone loves me. I bless everyone and everyone blesses me. I forgive everyone and everyone forgives me. I am loved, blessed, and forgiven. We are all free."

To Overcome Fear

- » "I cast this burden of fear on the CSO within, and I go free to be loving, happy, and harmonious, detached from the tyranny of fear."

- » "What universal power has done for others the CSO now does for me and more."

 » "I am guided and directed by the CSO's divine love and wisdom. I make right decisions quickly."

- » "There is nothing to fear, for the CSO makes my way clear and easy. There is nothing that can hurt."

> » "Only that which is for my highest and best good manifests in my life."

To Erase or Neutralize Mistakes

> » "I bless the past and forget it. I bless the future, knowing it is filled with wonderful opportunities and success. I live fully in the present now and am blessed with all I desire or require and more."

> » "Any seeming mistakes of my past are now transformed into my good."

> » "When I look at this situation in the rearview mirror of life, I will see how the CSO turned this situation into my good."

> » "I bless, love, and forgive everyone, and everyone blesses, loves, and forgives me. I bless, love, and forgive myself."

> » "There are no mistakes in the all-knowing power; therefore, there are no mistakes in my life."

To Realize Perfect Health

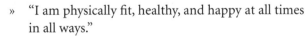

> » "I am physically fit, healthy, and happy at all times in all ways."

> » "I am growing increasingly more beautiful and healthy every day in every way."

» "As the perfect creation of the universe, my perfect health manifests. The CSO ensures my good health."

» "I am smarter, happier, healthier, and wealthier each and every moment of each and every day."

» "Every cell in my body is filled with universal healing light."

Suggested Inspirational Reading

Books that are suitable for the reading portion of the practice are listed below, but feel free to use any books that increase your receptivity to the understanding that the universal power is operating through us all.

As a Man Thinketh, James Allen, 1902

The Seven Spiritual Laws of Success: A Practical Guide to the Fulfillment of Your Dreams, Deepak Chopra, 1994

The Way of the Wizard: Twenty Spiritual Lessons for Creating the Life You Want, Deepak Chopra, 1997

The Power of Intention, Dr. Wayne W. Dyer, 2005

Think and Grow Rich, Napoleon Hill, 1937

The Power of Your Subconscious Mind, Joseph Murphy, 1963

The Dynamic Laws of Healing, Catherine Ponder, 1972

The Dynamic Laws of Prosperity, Catherine Ponder, 1962

The Four Agreements: A Practical Guide to Personal Freedom, Don Miguel Ruiz, 1997

The Game of Life and How to Play It, Florence Scovel Shinn, 1925

The Secret Door to Success, Florence Scovel Shinn, 1940

Your Word Is Your Wand, Florence Scovel Shinn, 1928

The Power of Now: A Guide to Spiritual Enlightenment, Eckhart Tolle, 1997

About the Author

Since 1982, May McCarthy has founded and grown six successful companies in a variety of industries as large as 250 employees and with over $100 million in annual revenues. She has also worked for Fortune 500 companies such as Johnson & Johnson and Boeing in sales and capital equipment purchasing, contracting, and barcode logistics design.

As part of McCarthy's passion for entrepreneurship, she is the chair of the board for the Seattle University Innovation and Entrepreneurship Center, an active angel investor, and an advisor to dozens of start-up companies. She also serves on boards for business, philanthropic, arts, and non-profit service organizations.

May McCarthy knows that her increasing success, fun, and growth are due to her partnership with the Divine. She meets daily with her CSO.

May McCarthy lives in Seattle with her husband Don Smith and their cat, Indy.

Learn more about May McCarthy here:

Facebook:

www.facebook.com/pages/May-Mccarthy/601413533280571

LinkedIn:

www.linkedin.com/pub/may-mccarthy/4/a55/b47/

Twitter:

www.twitter.com/maymcc

Hierophant Publishing
8301 Broadway, Suite 219
San Antonio, TX 78209
888-800-4240

www.hierophantpublishing.com

I'm so grateful for . . . .
Thank you

Celebrate the good fortunes
of others